GRIMMY™ Inc.

Goes Postal

by Mike Peters

TOR®

A TOM DOHERTY ASSOCIATES BOOK
NEW YORK

This is a work of fiction. All the characters and events portrayed in this book are either products of the author's imagination or are used fictitiously.

GRIMMY™ GOES POSTAL

Copyright © 2000 by Mike Peters

™ and copyright © 2000 by Grimmy, Inc. All rights reserved.

www.grimmy.com

This book contains material previously published in a trade edition as *Grimmy: The Horrors of Global Worming.*

A Tor Book
Published by Tom Doherty Associates, LLC
175 Fifth Avenue
New York, NY 10010

www.tor.com

Tor® is a registered trademark of Tom Doherty Associates, LLC.

ISBN: 0-812-54918-X

First edition: April 2000
First mass market edition: April 2001

Printed in the United States of America

0 9 8 7 6 5 4 3 2 1

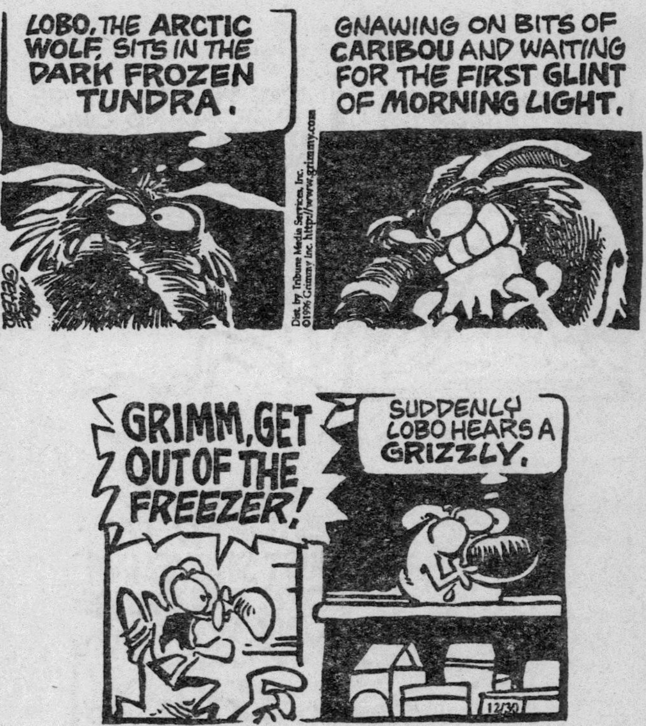
LOBO, THE ARCTIC WOLF, SITS IN THE DARK FROZEN TUNDRA.
GNAWING ON BITS OF CARIBOU AND WAITING FOR THE FIRST GLINT OF MORNING LIGHT.
Dist. by Tribune Media Services, Inc. ©1996 Grimmy Inc. http://www.grimmy.com
GRIMM, GET OUT OF THE FREEZER!
SUDDENLY LOBO HEARS A GRIZZLY.
12/30

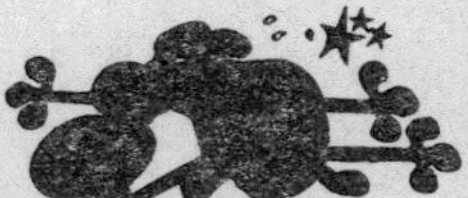

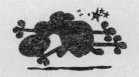

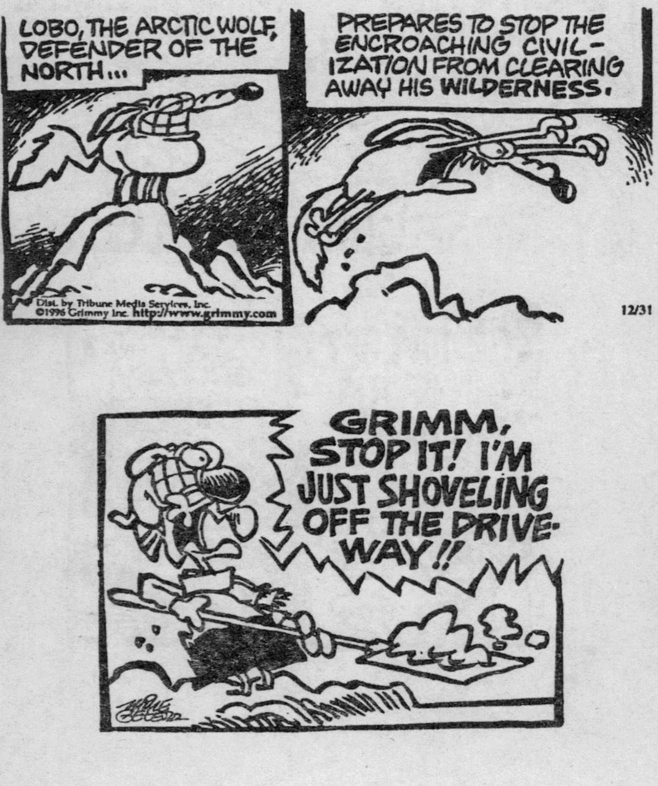
LOBO, THE ARCTIC WOLF, DEFENDER OF THE NORTH...
Dist. by Tribune Media Services, Inc.
©1996 Grimmy Inc. http://www.grimmy.com
PREPARES TO STOP THE ENCROACHING CIVIL-IZATION FROM CLEARING AWAY HIS WILDERNESS.
12/31
GRIMM, STOP IT! I'M JUST SHOVELING OFF THE DRIVE-WAY!!

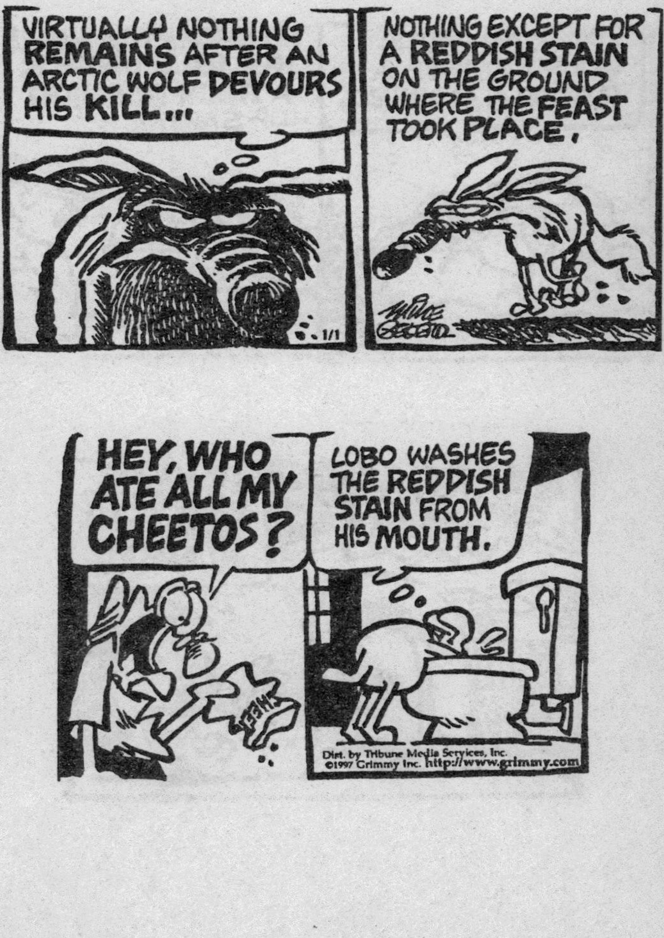
VIRTUALLY NOTHING REMAINS AFTER AN ARCTIC WOLF DEVOURS HIS KILL...
1/1
NOTHING EXCEPT FOR A REDDISH STAIN ON THE GROUND WHERE THE FEAST TOOK PLACE.
HEY, WHO ATE ALL MY CHEETOS?
LOBO WASHES THE REDDISH STAIN FROM HIS MOUTH.
Dist. by Tribune Media Services, Inc.
©1997 Grimmy Inc. http://www.grimmy.com

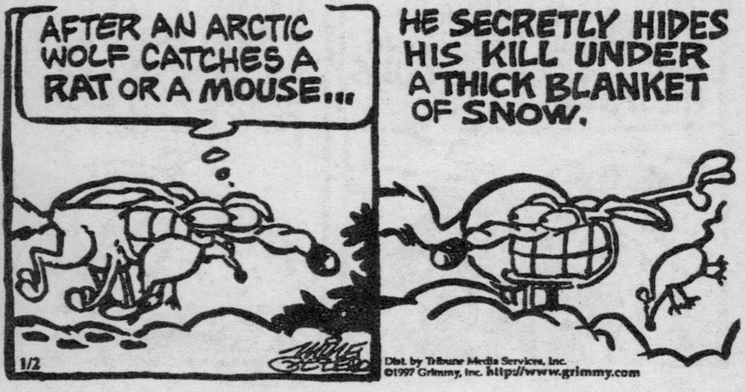
AFTER AN ARCTIC WOLF CATCHES A RAT OR A MOUSE...
1/2
HE SECRETLY HIDES HIS KILL UNDER A THICK BLANKET OF SNOW.

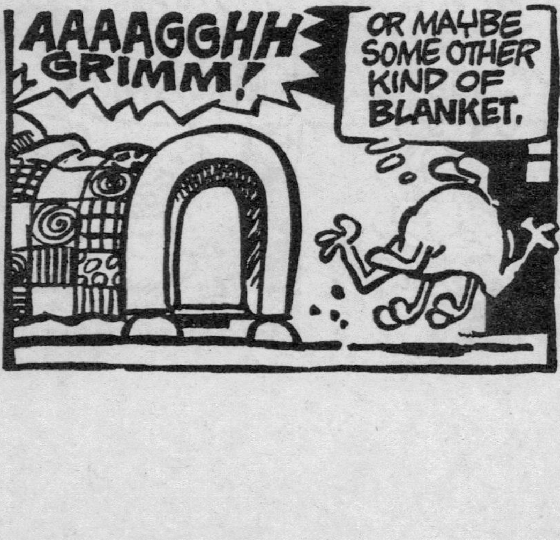
AAAAGGHH GRIMM!
OR MAYBE SOME OTHER KIND OF BLANKET.

WOLVES HELP PERFORM AN IMPORTANT *NATURAL* FUNCTION IN THE WILD.

THEY *STRENGTHEN* THE HERDS BY *ELIMINATING* THE *SICK* AND THE *OLD*.

OUCH! QUIT IT, GRIMM, YOU KNOW I'VE GOT A *COLD.*

CHOMP...

1/3

IN THE WINTER, WHEN THE DEER AND THE ANTELOPE ARE SCARCE...
ARCTIC WOLVES ARE FORCED TO LIVE ON A DIET OF MICE, RABBITS OR BIRDS...
Dist. by Tribune Media Services, Inc.
©1999 Grimmy, Inc. http://www.grimmy.com
OR SOMETIMES TWINKIES, DING DONGS AN' HO HO'S.
1/4

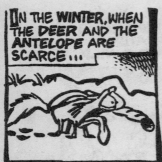

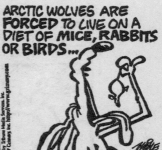

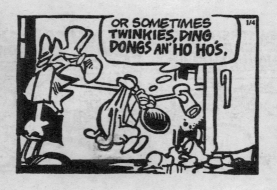

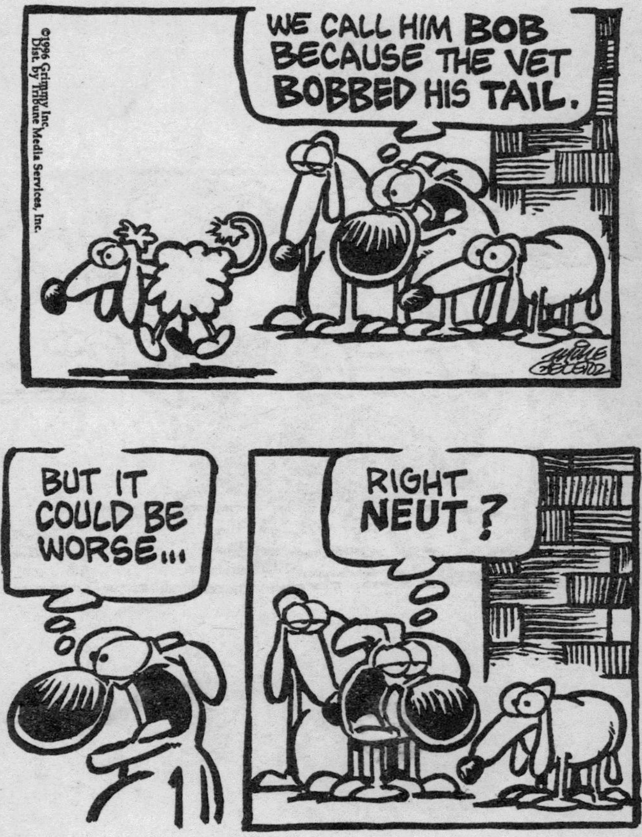
WE CALL HIM BOB BECAUSE THE VET BOBBED HIS TAIL.
©1996 Grimmy Inc. Dist. by TriBune Media Services, Inc.
BUT IT COULD BE WORSE...
RIGHT NEUT ?

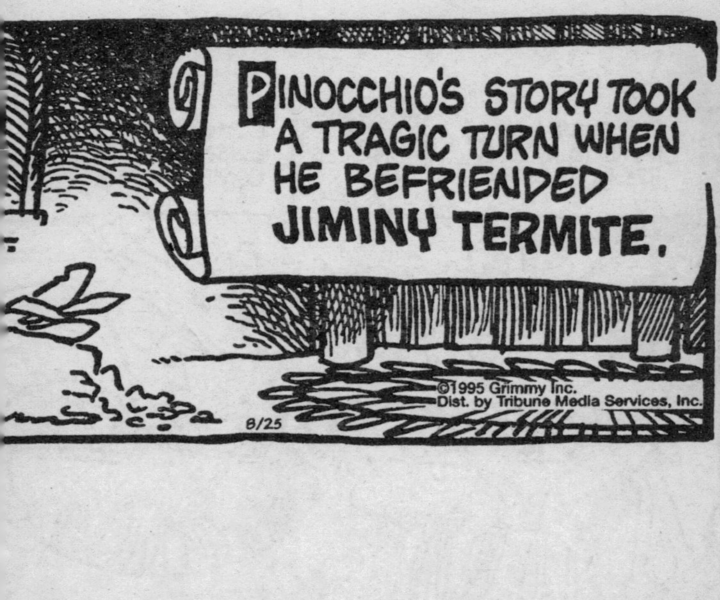
PINOCCHIO'S STORY TOOK A TRAGIC TURN WHEN HE BEFRIENDED JIMINY TERMITE.
©1995 Grimmy Inc.
Dist. by Tribune Media Services, Inc.
8/25

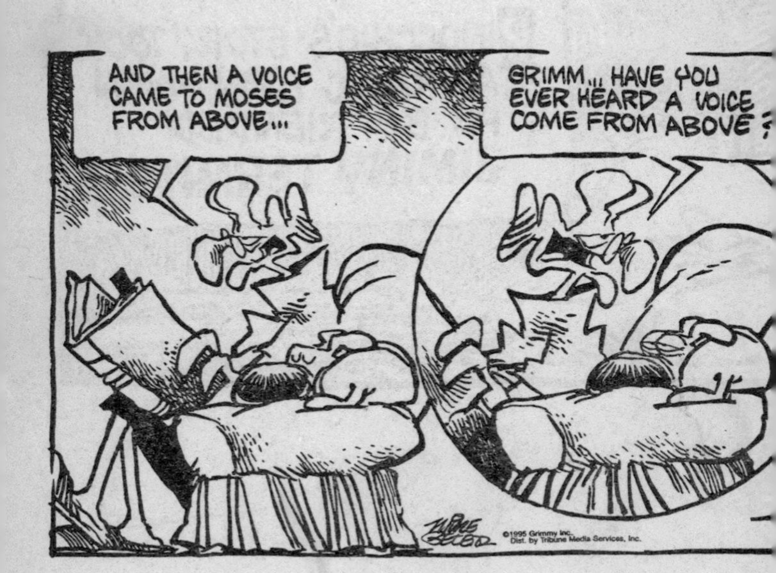
AND THEN A VOICE CAME TO MOSES FROM ABOVE...
GRIMM... HAVE YOU EVER HEARD A VOICE COME FROM ABOVE ?
©1995 Grimmy Inc. Dist. by Tribune Media Services, Inc.

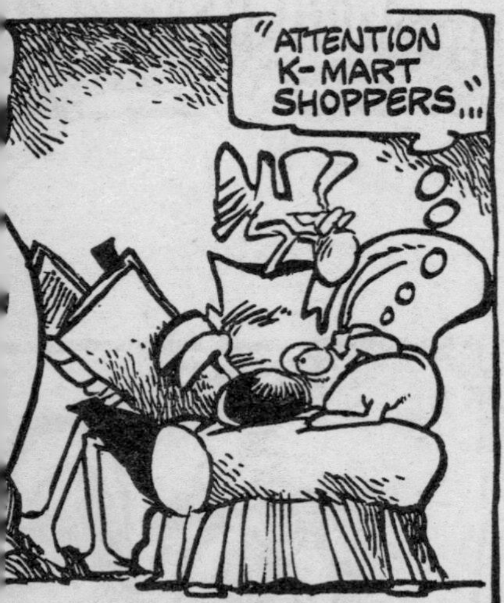
"ATTENTION K-MART SHOPPERS..."

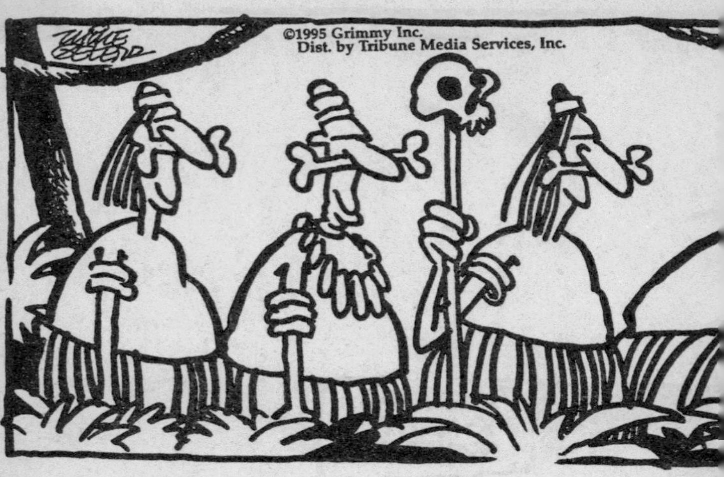
©1995 Grimmy Inc.
Dist. by Tribune Media Services, Inc.

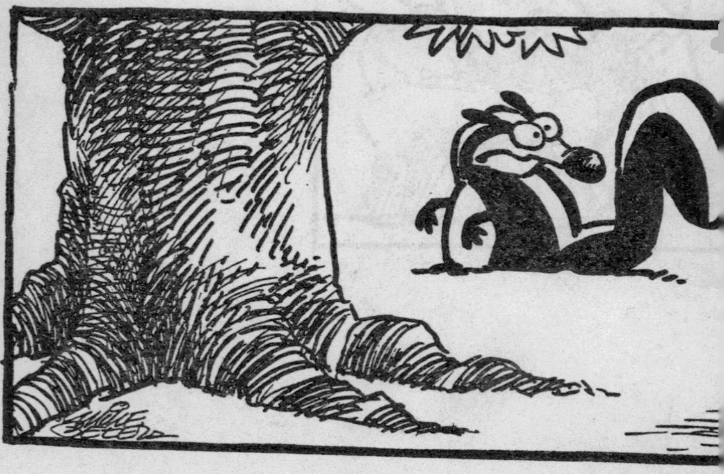

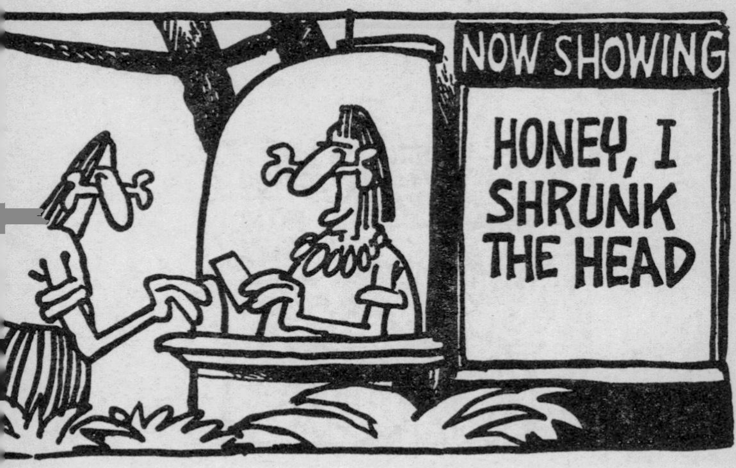
NOW SHOWING
HONEY, I SHRUNK THE HEAD

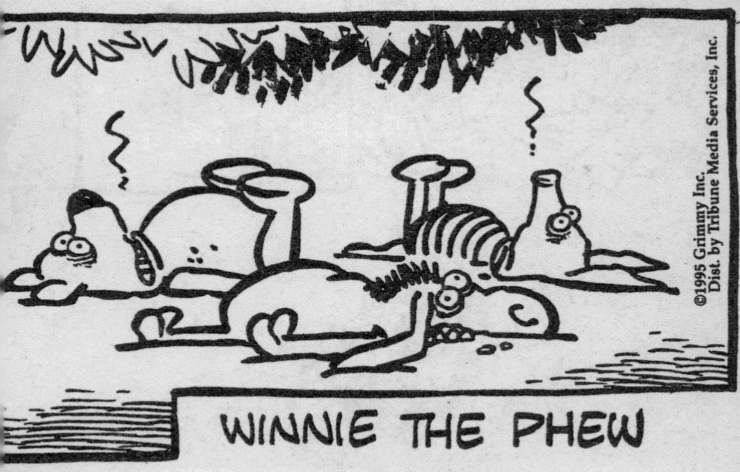
©1995 Grimmy Inc.
Dist. by Tribune Media Services, Inc.

WINNIE THE PHEW

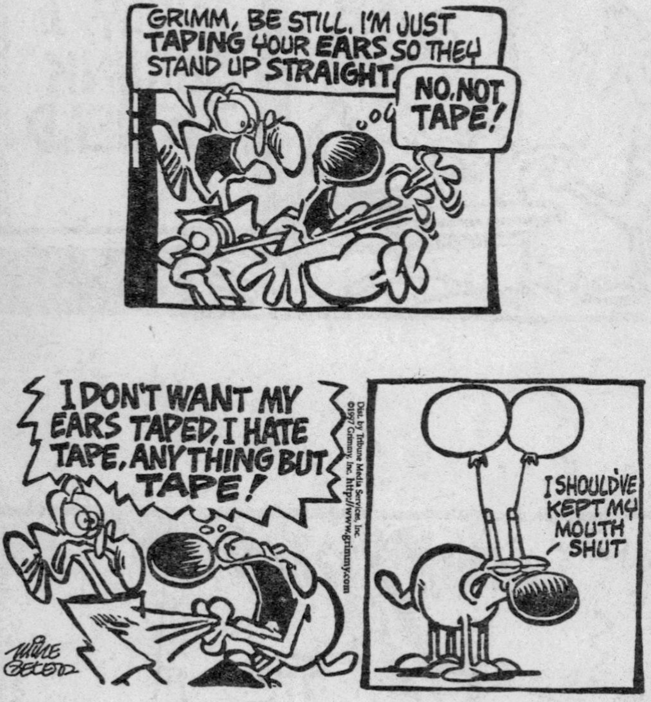
GRIMM, BE STILL. I'M JUST TAPING YOUR EARS SO THEY STAND UP STRAIGHT.
NO, NOT TAPE!
I DON'T WANT MY EARS TAPED, I HATE TAPE, ANYTHING BUT TAPE!
Dist. by Tribune Media Services, Inc. ©1997 Grimmy, Inc. http://www.grimmy.com
I SHOULD'VE KEPT MY MOUTH SHUT

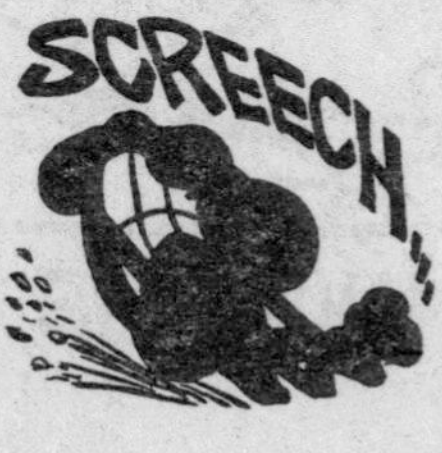
SCREECH...

I FEEL SO STUPID WITH MY EARS TAPED.
BE HONEST, ATTILA. WHAT DOES IT LOOK LIKE I HAVE ON MY HEAD?
MADONNA'S BRA.
Dist. by Tribune Media Services, Inc.
©1997 Grimmy, Inc. http://www.grimmy.com

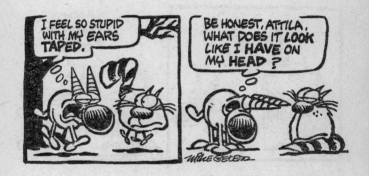

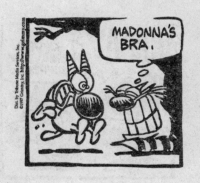

POP
Dist. by Tribune Media Services, Inc.
©1997 Grimmy, Inc. http://www.grimmy.com
WAAA!!
IF I SUFFER, EVERYBODY SUFFERS.

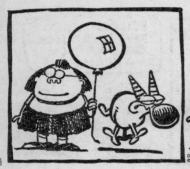

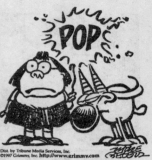

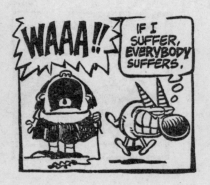

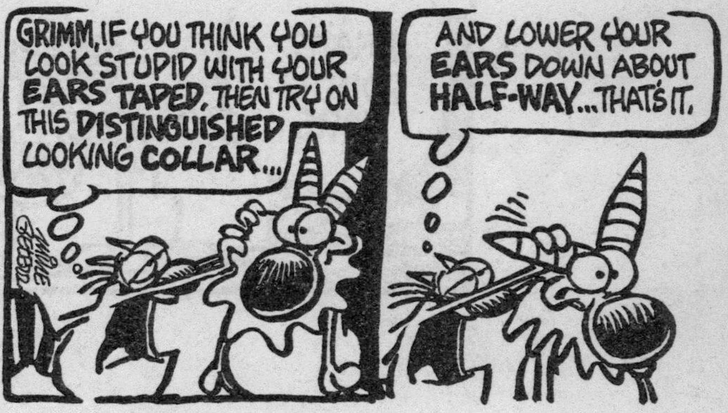
GRIMM, IF YOU THINK YOU LOOK STUPID WITH YOUR EARS TAPED, THEN TRY ON THIS DISTINGUISHED LOOKING COLLAR...
AND LOWER YOUR EARS DOWN ABOUT HALF-WAY...THAT'S IT.

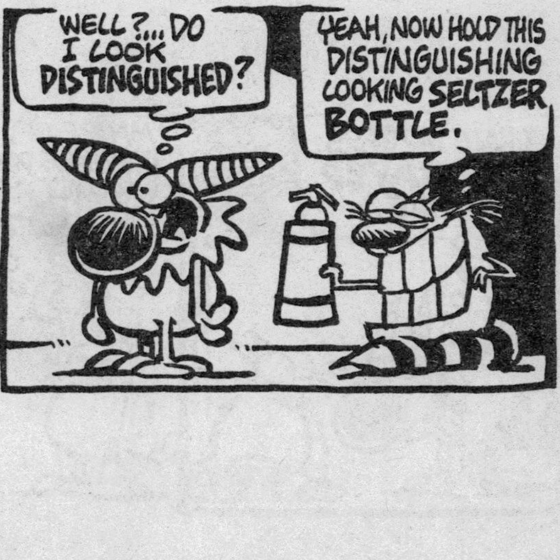
WELL?... DO I LOOK DISTINGUISHED?
YEAH, NOW HOLD THIS DISTINGUISHING LOOKING SELTZER BOTTLE.

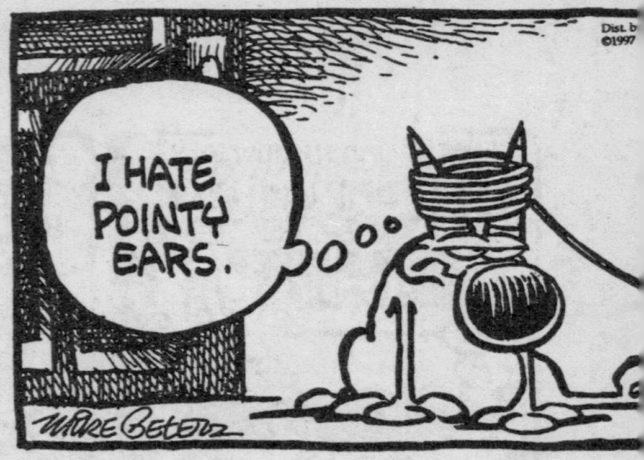
I HATE POINTY EARS.
Dist. b
©1997
MARK BELETZ

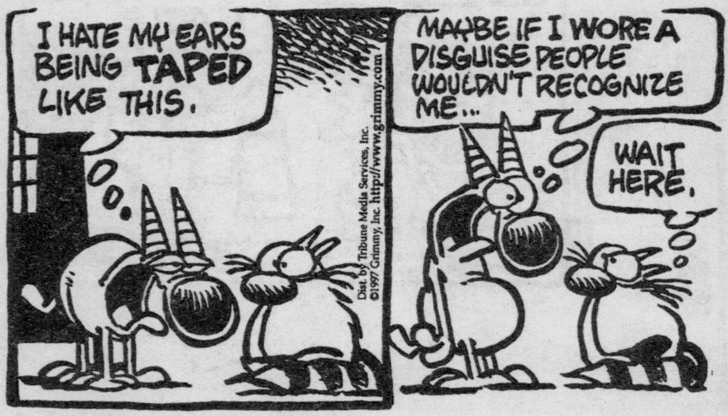
I HATE MY EARS BEING **TAPED** LIKE THIS.
Dist. by Tribune Media Services, Inc.
©1997 Grimmy, Inc. http://www.grimmy.com
MAYBE IF I WORE A DISGUISE PEOPLE WOULDN'T RECOGNIZE ME...
WAIT HERE.

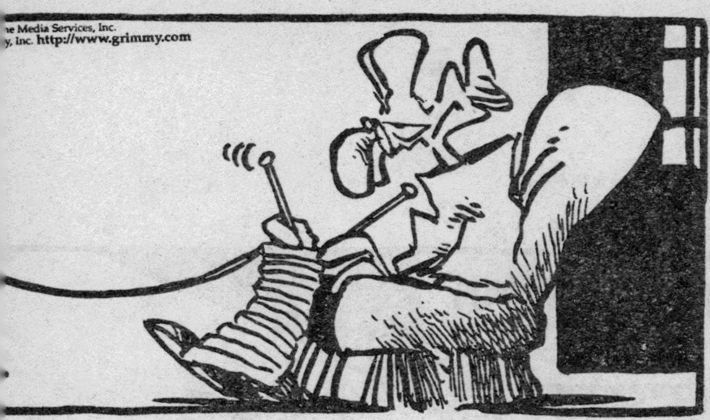
ne Media Services, Inc.
y, Inc. http://www.grimmy.com

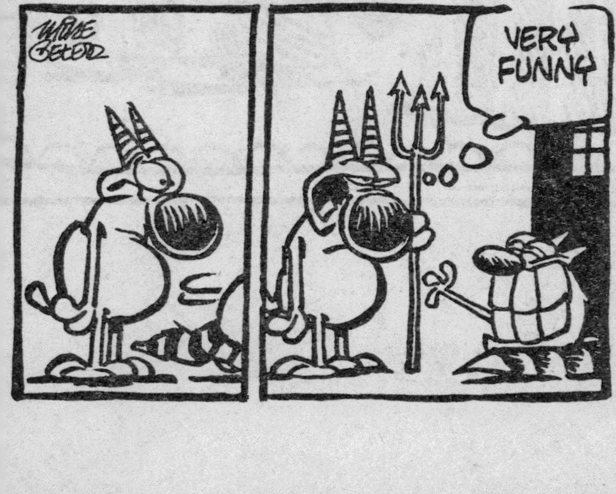
VERY FUNNY

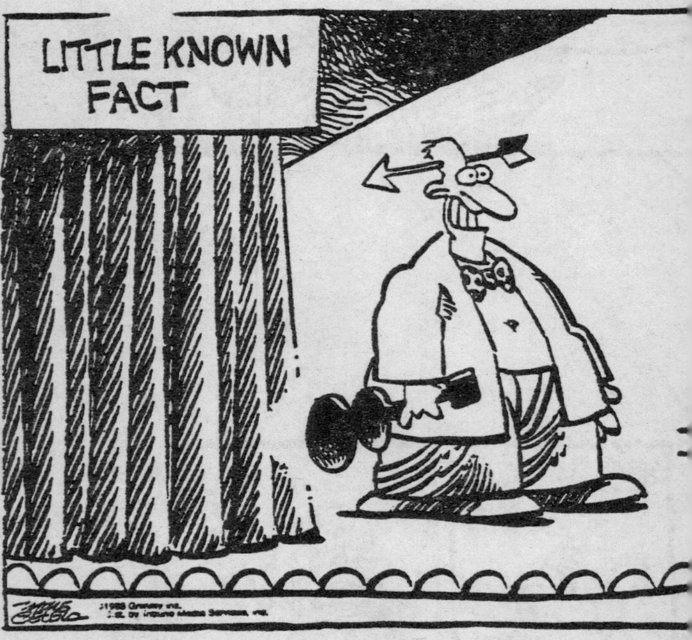
LITTLE KNOWN FACT

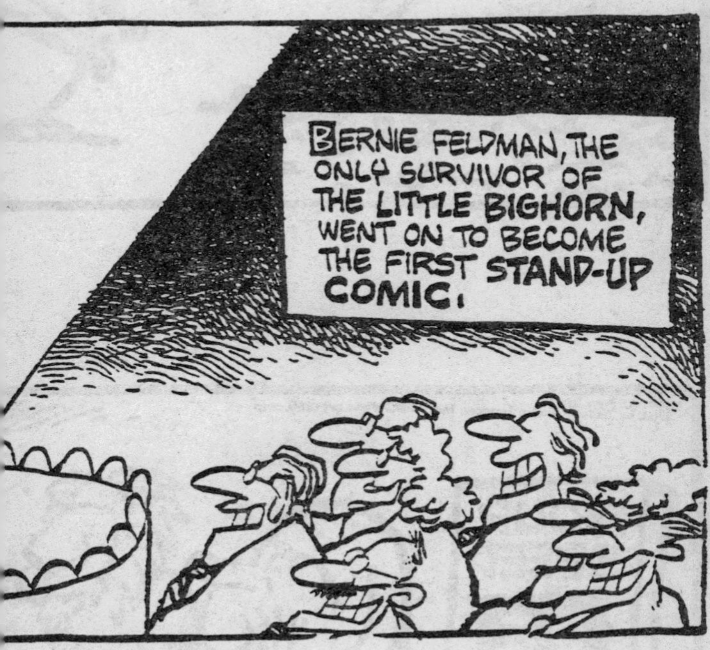
BERNIE FELDMAN, THE ONLY SURVIVOR OF THE LITTLE BIGHORN, WENT ON TO BECOME THE FIRST STAND-UP COMIC.

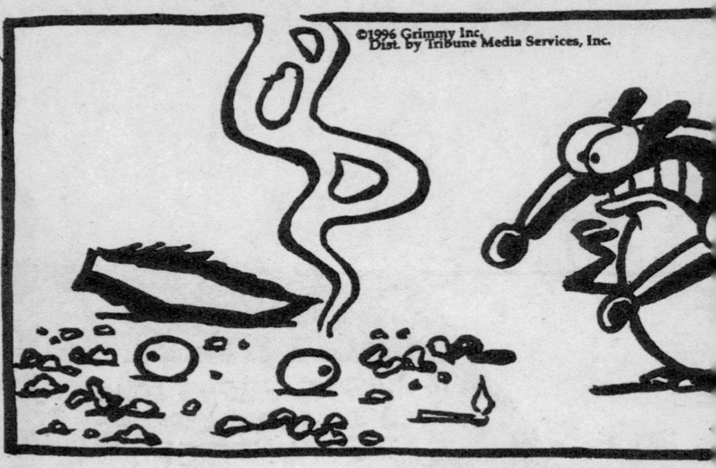
©1996 Grimmy Inc.
Dist. by Tribune Media Services, Inc.

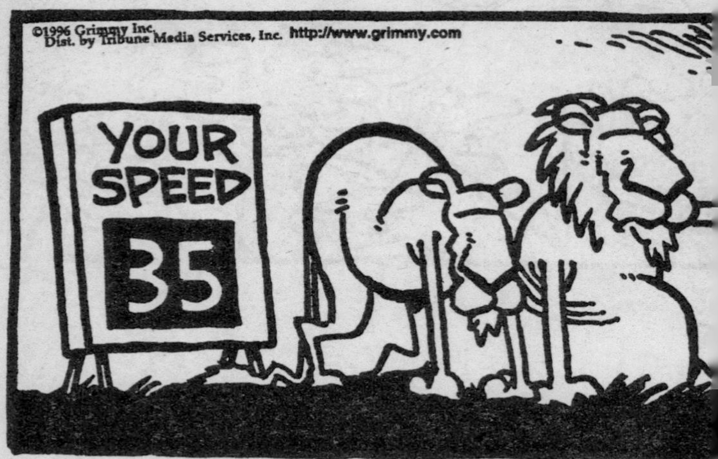
©1996 Grimmy Inc.
Dist. by Tribune Media Services, Inc. http://www.grimmy.com
YOUR SPEED
35

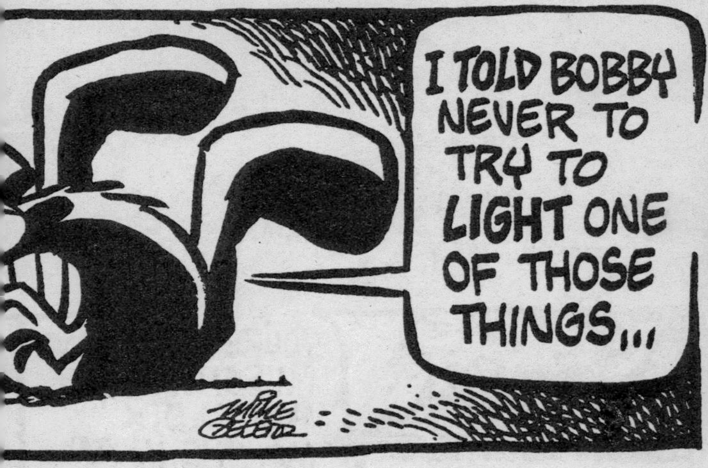
I TOLD BOBBY NEVER TO TRY TO LIGHT ONE OF THOSE THINGS...

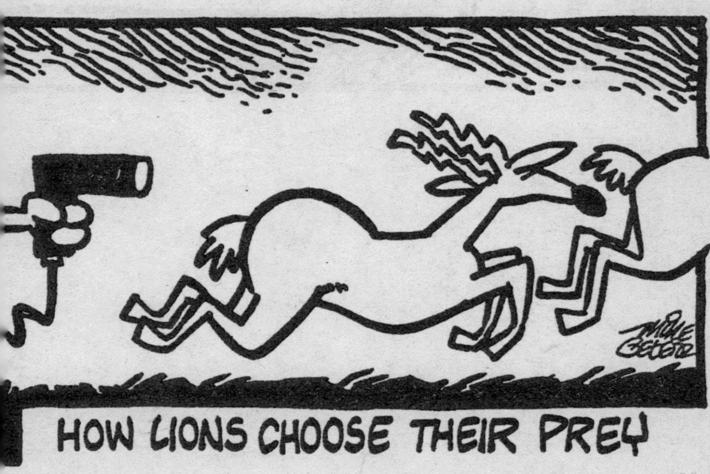

HOW LIONS CHOOSE THEIR PREY

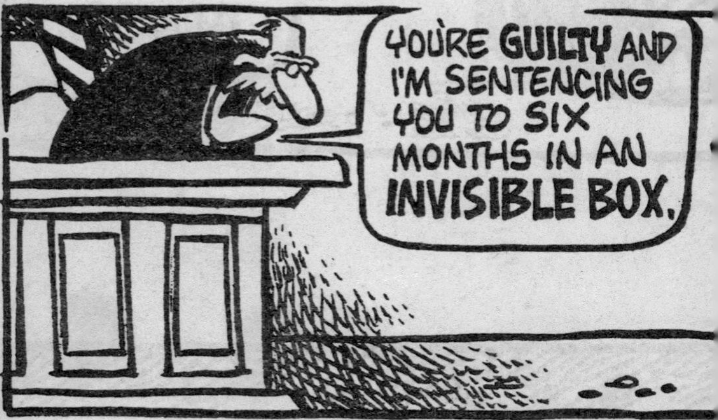
YOU'RE GUILTY AND I'M SENTENCING YOU TO SIX MONTHS IN AN INVISIBLE BOX.

MIME
COURT

©1996 Grimmy Inc.
Dist. by Tribune Media Services, Inc.

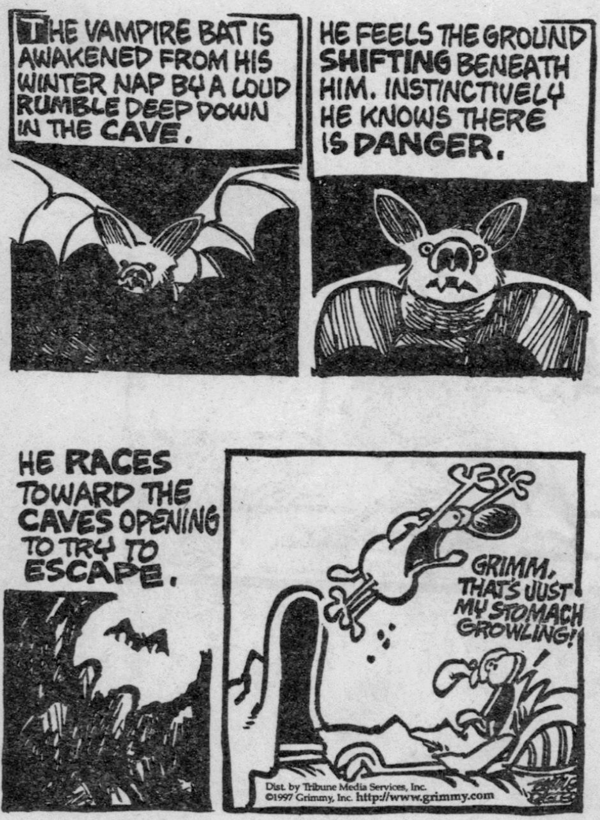
THE VAMPIRE BAT IS AWAKENED FROM HIS WINTER NAP BY A LOUD RUMBLE DEEP DOWN IN THE CAVE.
HE FEELS THE GROUND SHIFTING BENEATH HIM. INSTINCTIVELY HE KNOWS THERE IS DANGER.
HE RACES TOWARD THE CAVES OPENING TO TRY TO ESCAPE.
GRIMM, THAT'S JUST MY STOMACH GROWLING!
Dist. by Tribune Media Services, Inc.
©1997 Grimmy, Inc. http://www.grimmy.com

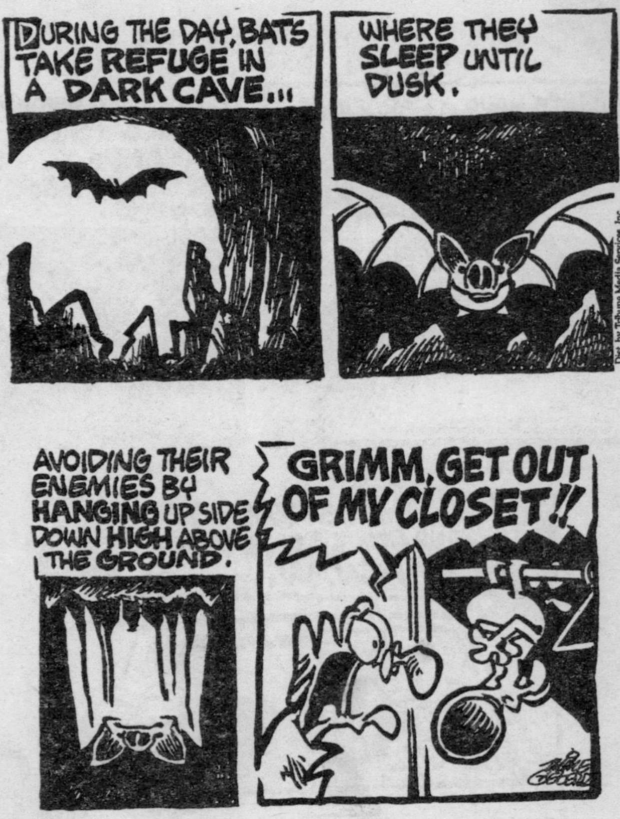
DURING THE DAY, BATS TAKE REFUGE IN A DARK CAVE...
WHERE THEY SLEEP UNTIL DUSK.
AVOIDING THEIR ENEMIES BY HANGING UP SIDE DOWN HIGH ABOVE THE GROUND.
GRIMM, GET OUT OF MY CLOSET!!

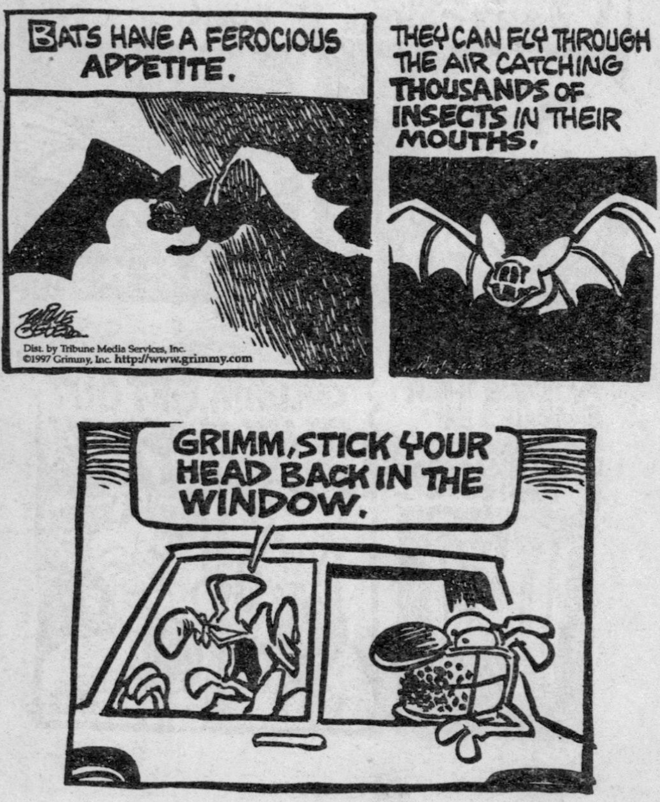

BATS HAVE A FEROCIOUS APPETITE.
Dist. by Tribune Media Services, Inc.
©1997 Grimmy, Inc. http://www.grimmy.com
THEY CAN FLY THROUGH THE AIR CATCHING THOUSANDS OF INSECTS IN THEIR MOUTHS.
GRIMM, STICK YOUR HEAD BACK IN THE WINDOW.

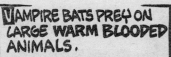

VAMPIRE BATS PREY ON LARGE WARM BLOODED ANIMALS.

BATS HAVE SHARP TRIANGULAR SHAPED TEETH THAT CUT LIKE A RAZOR.

HE SWOOPS DOWN TO SUCK THE RED LIQUID FROM THE UNSUSPECTING VICTIM.

SSLLUU RRRPP.

HEY, THAT'S MY STRAWBERRY SUNDAE.

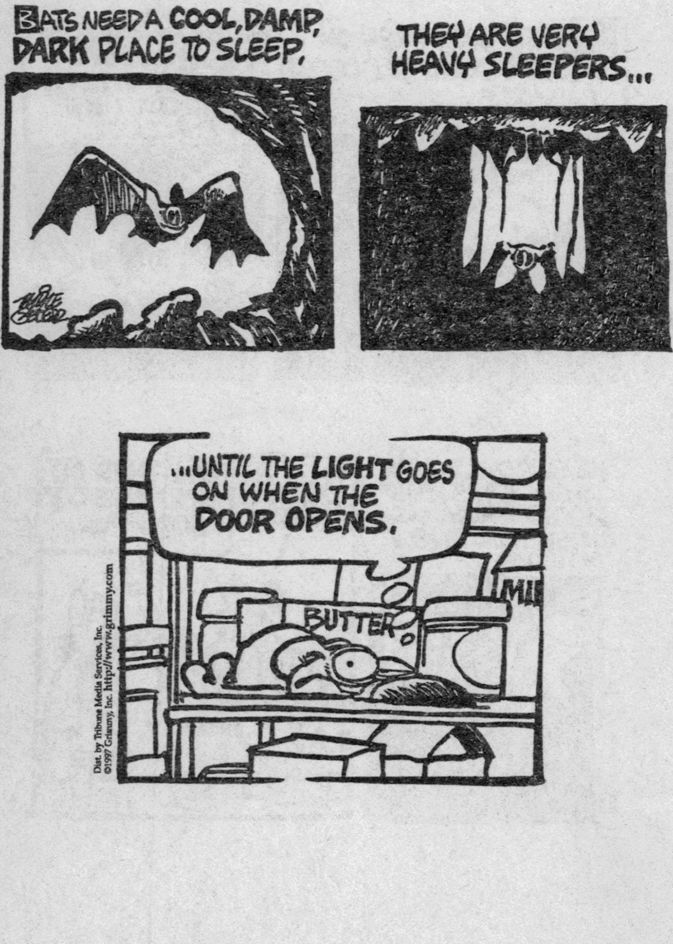
BATS NEED A COOL, DAMP, DARK PLACE TO SLEEP.
THEY ARE VERY HEAVY SLEEPERS...
...UNTIL THE LIGHT GOES ON WHEN THE DOOR OPENS.
BUTTER

KNOCK KNOCK
I'LL GET IT.
AAAGH!
SLAM!
Dist. by Tribune Media Services, Inc.
©1997 Grimmy, Inc. http://www.grimmy.com
GRIMMY, WHO WAS IT?
PAT BOONE!

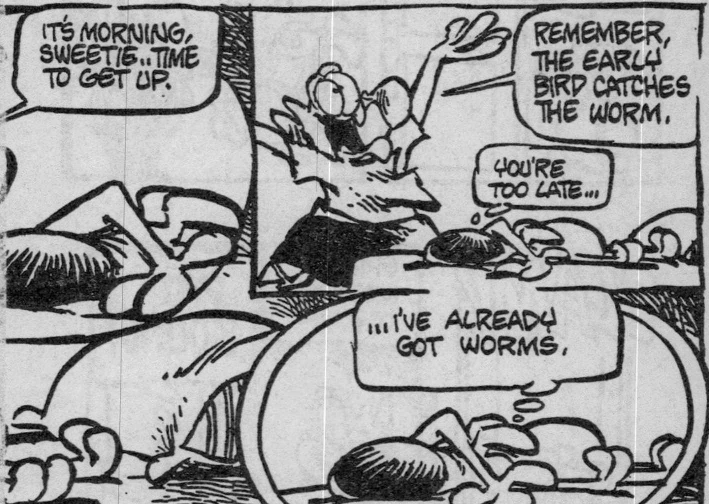
IT'S MORNING, SWEETIE.. TIME TO GET UP.
REMEMBER, THE EARLY BIRD CATCHES THE WORM.
YOU'RE TOO LATE...
...I'VE ALREADY GOT WORMS.

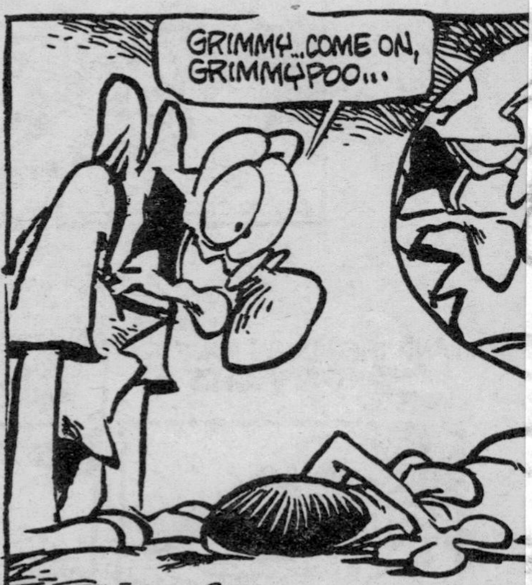
GRIMMY...COME ON, GRIMMYPOO...

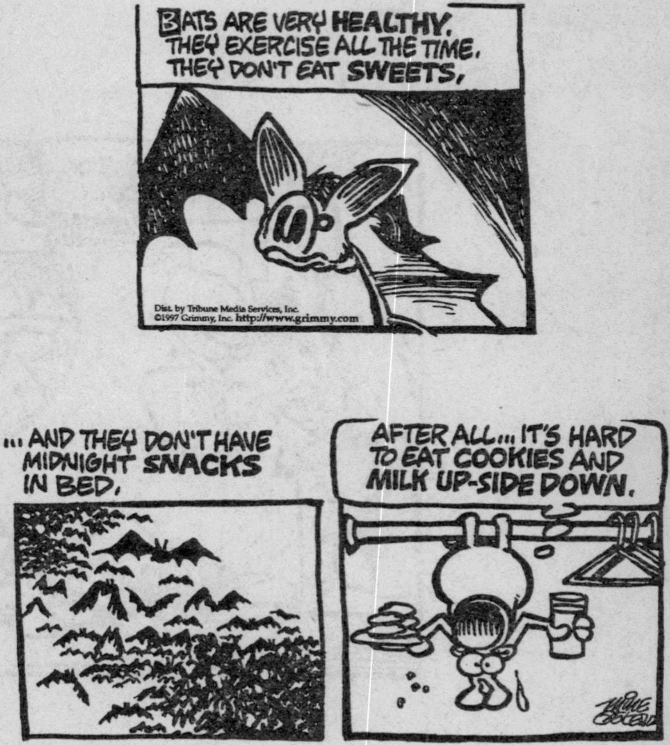
BATS ARE VERY HEALTHY. THEY EXERCISE ALL THE TIME. THEY DON'T EAT SWEETS,
Dist. by Tribune Media Services, Inc.
©1997 Grimmy, Inc. http://www.grimmy.com
... AND THEY DON'T HAVE MIDNIGHT SNACKS IN BED,
AFTER ALL... IT'S HARD TO EAT COOKIES AND MILK UP-SIDE DOWN.

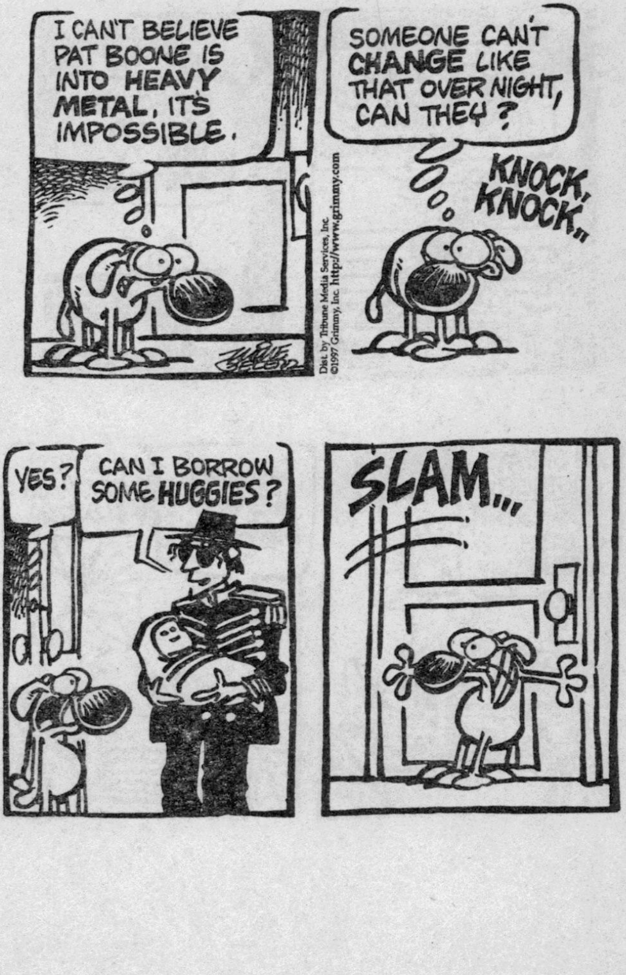
I CAN'T BELIEVE PAT BOONE IS INTO HEAVY METAL, IT'S IMPOSSIBLE.
SOMEONE CAN'T CHANGE LIKE THAT OVER NIGHT, CAN THEY?
KNOCK, KNOCK..
Dist. by Tribune Media Services, Inc.
©1997 Grimmy, Inc. http://www.grimmy.com
YES?
CAN I BORROW SOME HUGGIES?
SLAM...

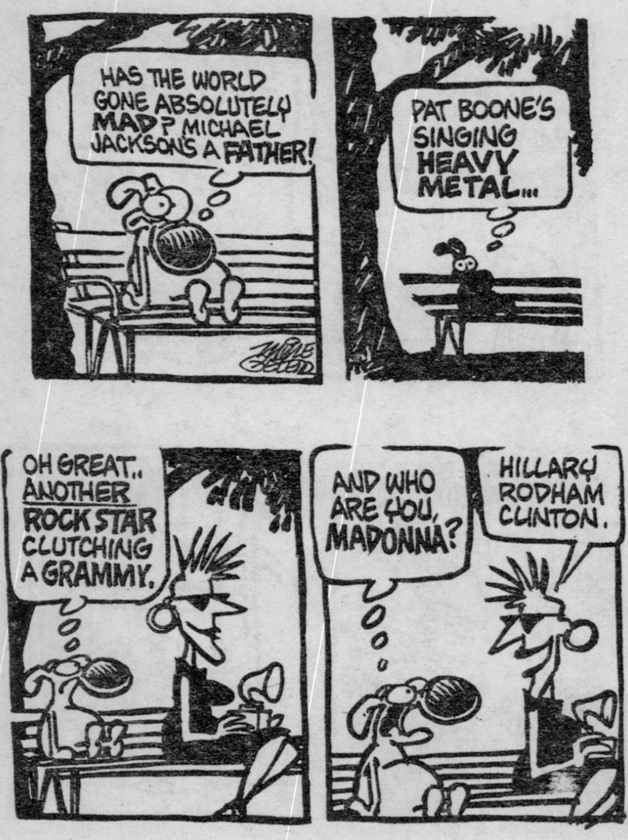
HAS THE WORLD GONE ABSOLUTELY MAD? MICHAEL JACKSON'S A FATHER!
PAT BOONE'S SINGING HEAVY METAL...
OH GREAT.. ANOTHER ROCK STAR CLUTCHING A GRAMMY.
AND WHO ARE YOU, MADONNA?
HILLARY RODHAM CLINTON.

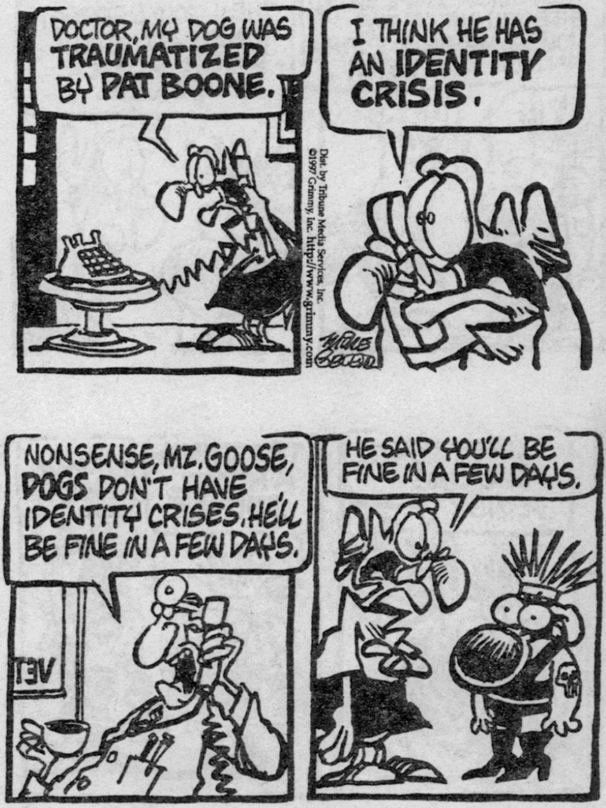
DOCTOR, MY DOG WAS TRAUMATIZED BY PAT BOONE.
I THINK HE HAS AN IDENTITY CRISIS.
Dist. by Tribune Media Services, Inc. ©1997 Grimmy, Inc. http://www.grimmy.com
NONSENSE, MZ. GOOSE, DOGS DON'T HAVE IDENTITY CRISES. HE'LL BE FINE IN A FEW DAYS.
VET
HE SAID YOU'LL BE FINE IN A FEW DAYS.

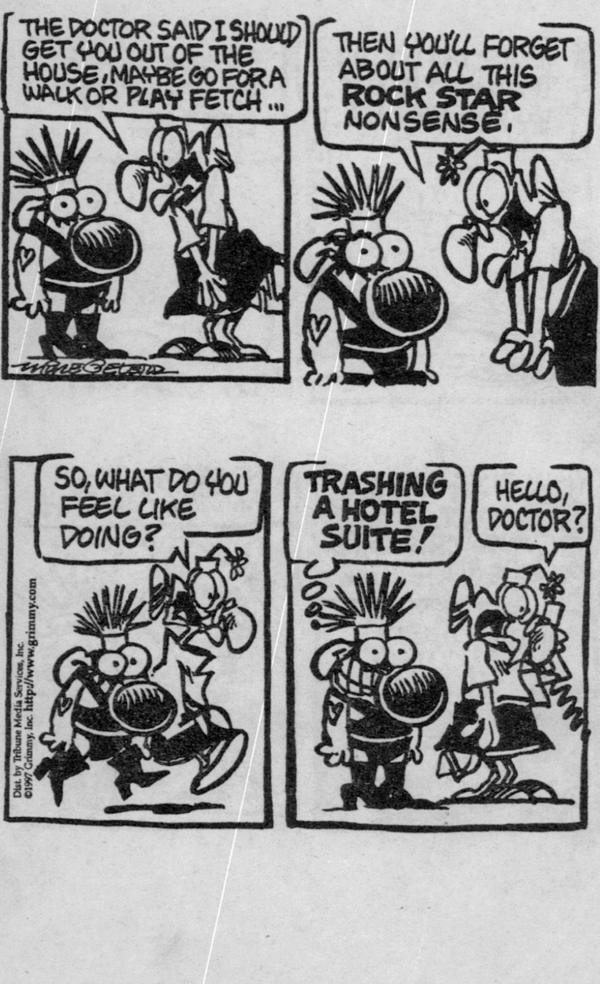
THE DOCTOR SAID I SHOULD GET YOU OUT OF THE HOUSE, MAYBE GO FOR A WALK OR PLAY FETCH...
THEN YOU'LL FORGET ABOUT ALL THIS ROCK STAR NONSENSE.
SO, WHAT DO YOU FEEL LIKE DOING?
Dist. by Tribune Media Services, Inc. ©1997 Grimmy, Inc. http://www.grimmy.com
TRASHING A HOTEL SUITE!
HELLO, DOCTOR?

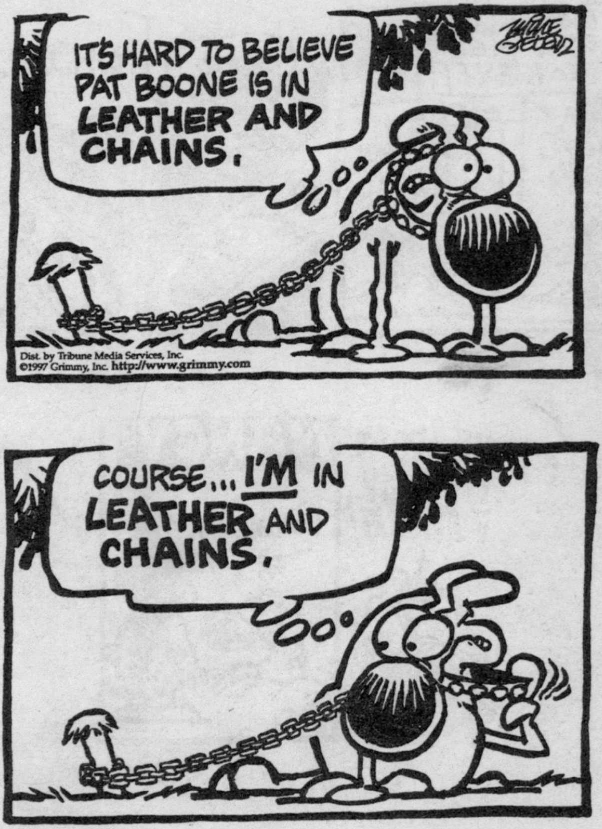
IT'S HARD TO BELIEVE PAT BOONE IS IN LEATHER AND CHAINS.
Dist. by Tribune Media Services, Inc.
©1997 Grimmy, Inc. http://www.grimmy.com
COURSE... I'M IN LEATHER AND CHAINS.

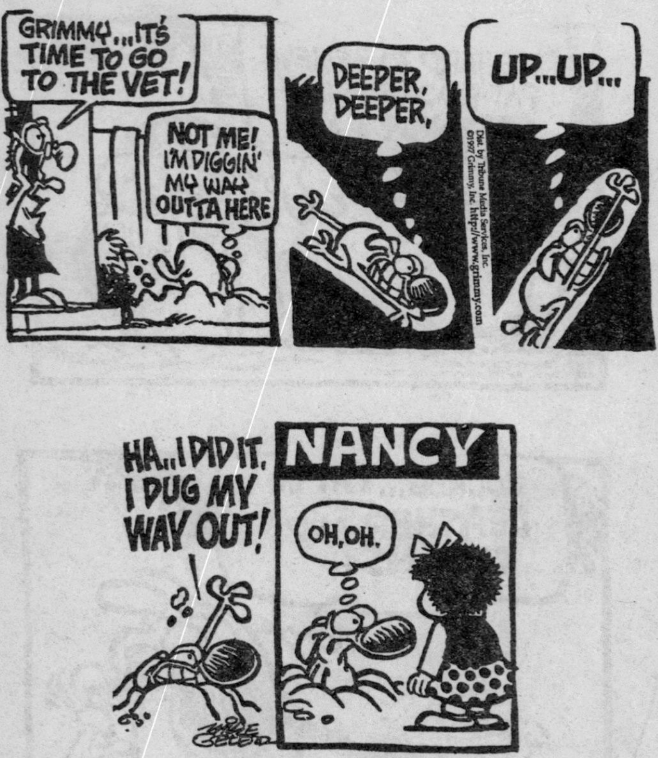
GRIMMY...IT'S TIME TO GO TO THE VET!
NOT ME! I'M DIGGIN' MY WAY OUTTA HERE
DEEPER, DEEPER,
Dist. by Tribune Media Services, Inc. ©1997 Grimmy, Inc. http://www.grimmy.com
UP...UP...
HA..I DID IT. I DUG MY WAY OUT!
NANCY
OH,OH.

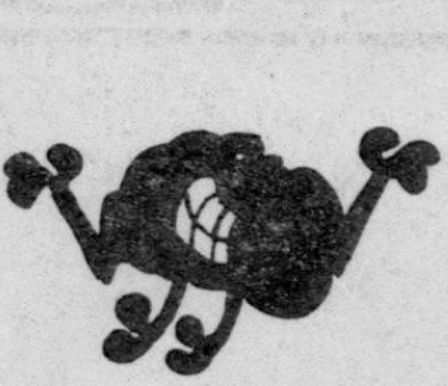

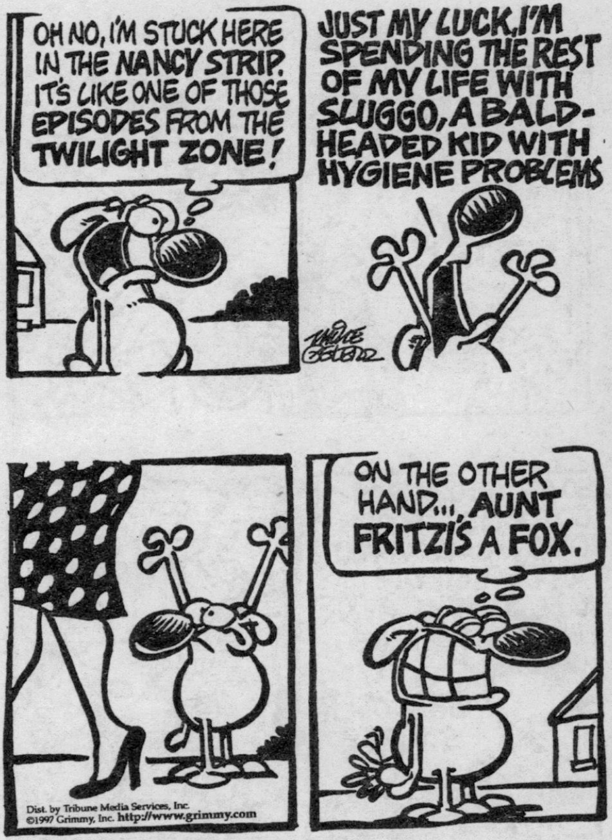
OH NO, I'M STUCK HERE IN THE NANCY STRIP. IT'S LIKE ONE OF THOSE EPISODES FROM THE TWILIGHT ZONE!
JUST MY LUCK, I'M SPENDING THE REST OF MY LIFE WITH SLUGGO, A BALD-HEADED KID WITH HYGIENE PROBLEMS
Dist. by Tribune Media Services, Inc.
©1997 Grimmy, Inc. http://www.grimmy.com
ON THE OTHER HAND..., AUNT FRITZI'S A FOX.

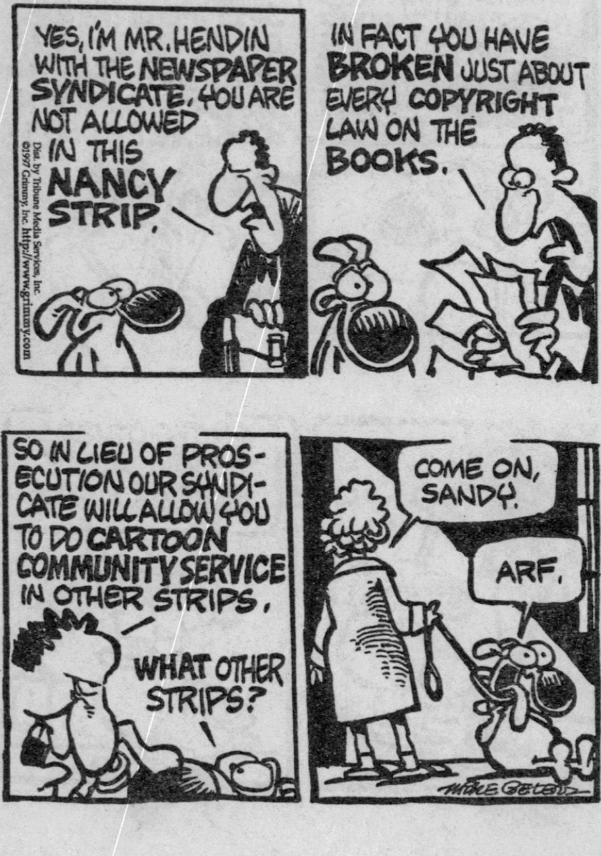
YES, I'M MR. HENDIN WITH THE NEWSPAPER SYNDICATE. YOU ARE NOT ALLOWED IN THIS NANCY STRIP.
Dist. by Tribune Media Services, Inc
©1997 Grimmy, Inc. http://www.grimmy.com
IN FACT YOU HAVE BROKEN JUST ABOUT EVERY COPYRIGHT LAW ON THE BOOKS.
SO IN LIEU OF PROSECUTION OUR SYNDICATE WILL ALLOW YOU TO DO CARTOON COMMUNITY SERVICE IN OTHER STRIPS.
WHAT OTHER STRIPS?
COME ON, SANDY.
ARF.

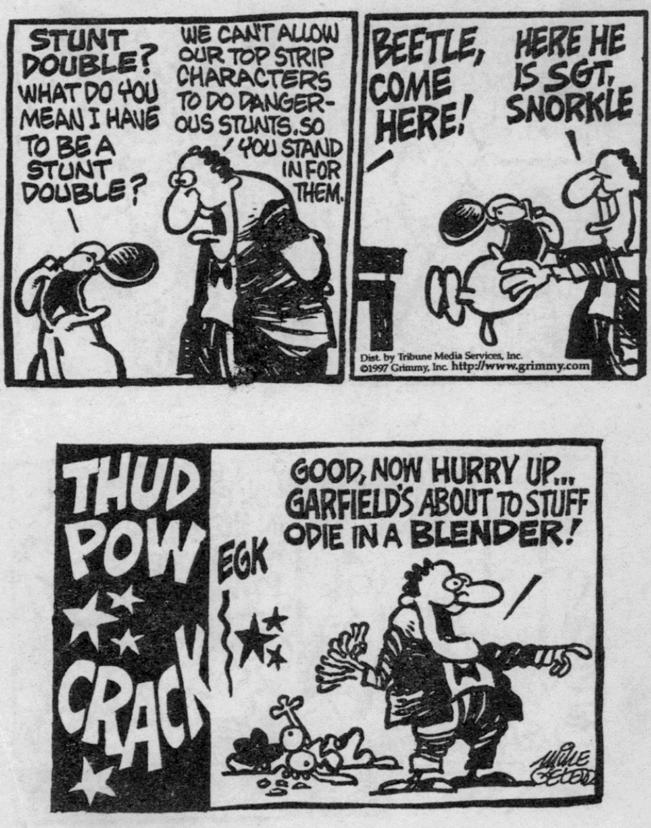
STUNT DOUBLE? WHAT DO YOU MEAN I HAVE TO BE A STUNT DOUBLE?
WE CAN'T ALLOW OUR TOP STRIP CHARACTERS TO DO DANGEROUS STUNTS. SO YOU STAND IN FOR THEM.
BEETLE, COME HERE!
HERE HE IS SGT. SNORKLE
Dist. by Tribune Media Services, Inc.
©1997 Grimmy, Inc. http://www.grimmy.com
THUD
POW
CRACK
EGK
GOOD, NOW HURRY UP... GARFIELD'S ABOUT TO STUFF ODIE IN A BLENDER!

GRIMM, THE SYNDICATE HAS A FULL DAY OF CARTOON STUNTS FOR YOU TO DO.
LET'S SEE, AT 2 O'CLOCK YOU GET PUNCHED OUT BY POPEYE, THEN YOU'RE IN A BAR FIGHT WITH ANDY CAPP THEN...
WHOOSH
OH, I FORGOT, FIRST YOU GET COVERED IN HOT OIL BY HAGAR THEN POPEYE...

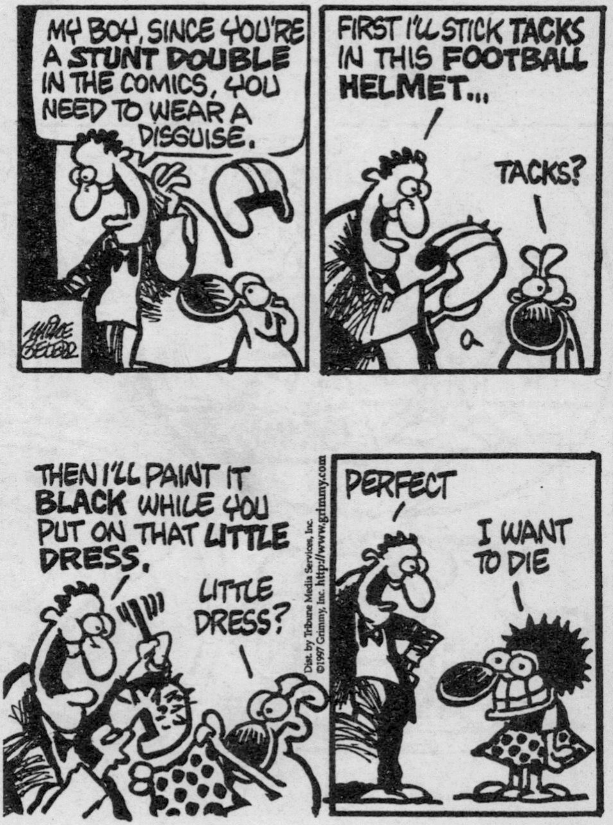
MY BOY, SINCE YOU'RE A STUNT DOUBLE IN THE COMICS, YOU NEED TO WEAR A DISGUISE.
FIRST I'LL STICK TACKS IN THIS FOOTBALL HELMET...
TACKS?
THEN I'LL PAINT IT BLACK WHILE YOU PUT ON THAT LITTLE DRESS.
LITTLE DRESS?
Dist. by Tribune Media Services, Inc. ©1997 Grimmy, Inc. http://www.grimmy.com
PERFECT
I WANT TO DIE

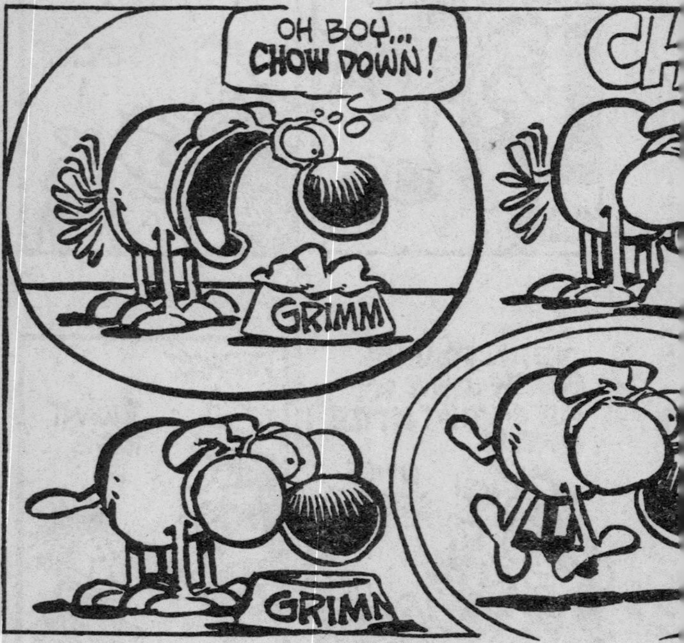
OH BOY...
CHOW DOWN!
GRIMM

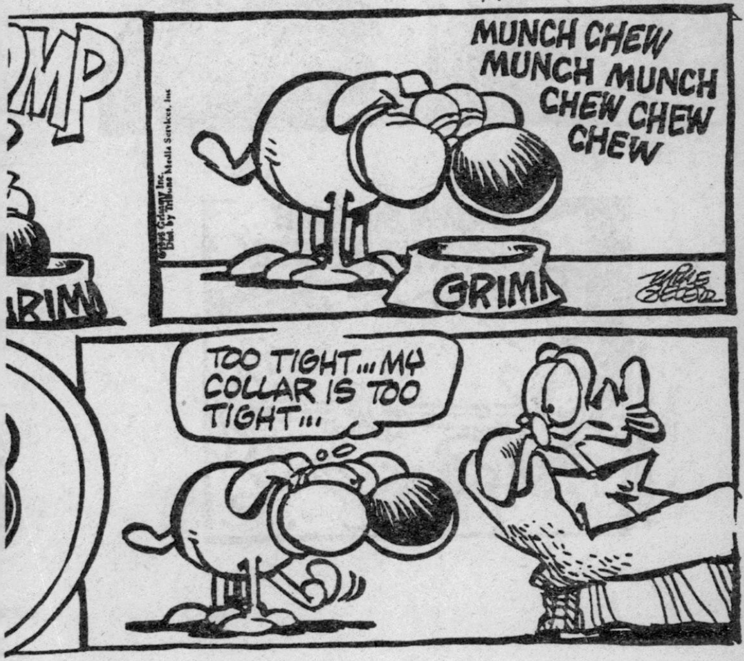
MUNCH CHEW MUNCH MUNCH CHEW CHEW CHEW
GRIM
TOO TIGHT... MY COLLAR IS TOO TIGHT...

THE MALE WOLF MUST HAVE COMPLETE CONTROL OF HIS LIFE.

HE CALLS THE SHOTS. NOBODY MAKES IMPORTANT DECISIONS FOR HIM.

GRIMM, GIVE ME BACK THE REMOTE!

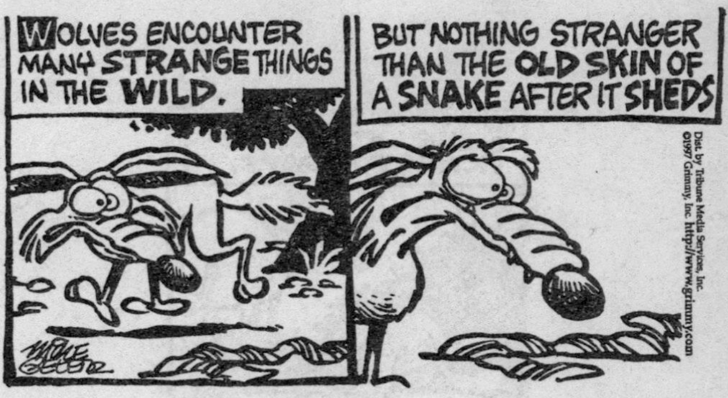
WOLVES ENCOUNTER MANY STRANGE THINGS IN THE WILD.
BUT NOTHING STRANGER THAN THE OLD SKIN OF A SNAKE AFTER IT SHEDS
Dist. by Tribune Media Services, Inc.
©1997 Grimmy, Inc. http://www.grimmy.com

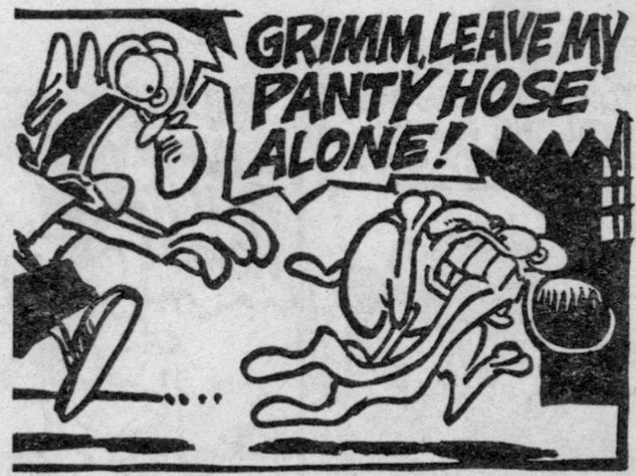
GRIMM, LEAVE MY PANTY HOSE ALONE!

WOLVES NEVER GIVE UP, THEY WILL STALK THEIR VICTIMS FOR DAYS.
PATIENTLY FOLLOWING THE PREY UNTIL THE RIGHT MOMENT TO ATTACK.
Dist. by Tribune Media Services, Inc.
©1997 Grimmy, Inc http://www.grimmy.com
YOU HEARD ME! YOUR STUPID YELLOW DOG FOLLOWED ME HOME!
US
MAIL

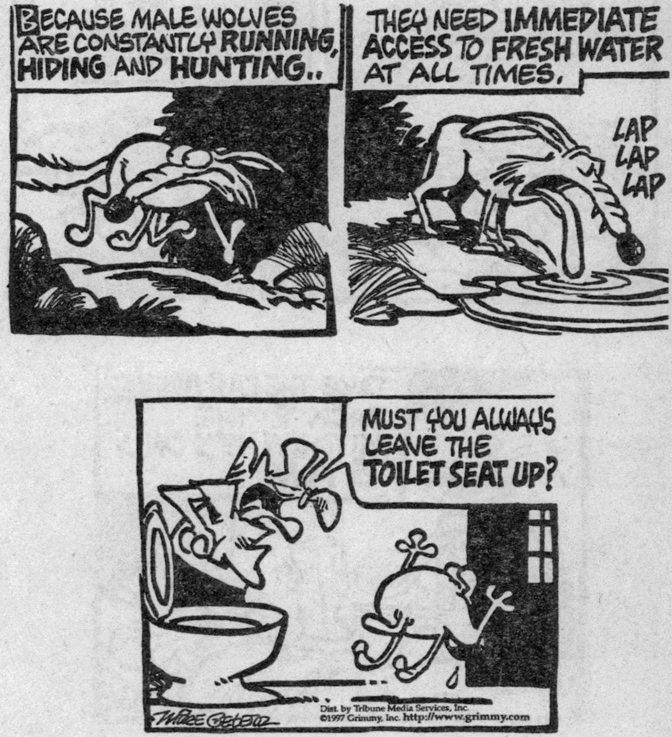
BECAUSE MALE WOLVES ARE CONSTANTLY RUNNING, HIDING AND HUNTING..
THEY NEED IMMEDIATE ACCESS TO FRESH WATER AT ALL TIMES.
LAP LAP LAP
MUST YOU ALWAYS LEAVE THE TOILET SEAT UP?
Dist. by Tribune Media Services, Inc.
©1997 Grimmy, Inc. http://www.grimmy.com

WOLVES RELY ON EACH OTHER TO SHARE THE HUNTING DUTIES.
WHEN THE PACK GETS HUNGRY, THEY GO ALL OUT TO FEED THEMSELVES.
Dist. by Tribune Media Services, Inc.
©1997 Grimmy, Inc. http://www.grimmy.com
TAKE THE CAN OPENER BACK TO THE KITCHEN, IT'S ONLY 5 A.M.

WOLVES HAVE AN AMAZING SENSE OF SMELL.
Dist. by Tribune Media Services, Inc.
©1997 Grimmy, Inc. http://www.grimmy.com
THEY CAN FIND FOOD ANYWHERE, NO MATTER HOW DEEP IT'S BURIED.
THREE CHEETOS AND A TOOTSIE ROLL BAR.

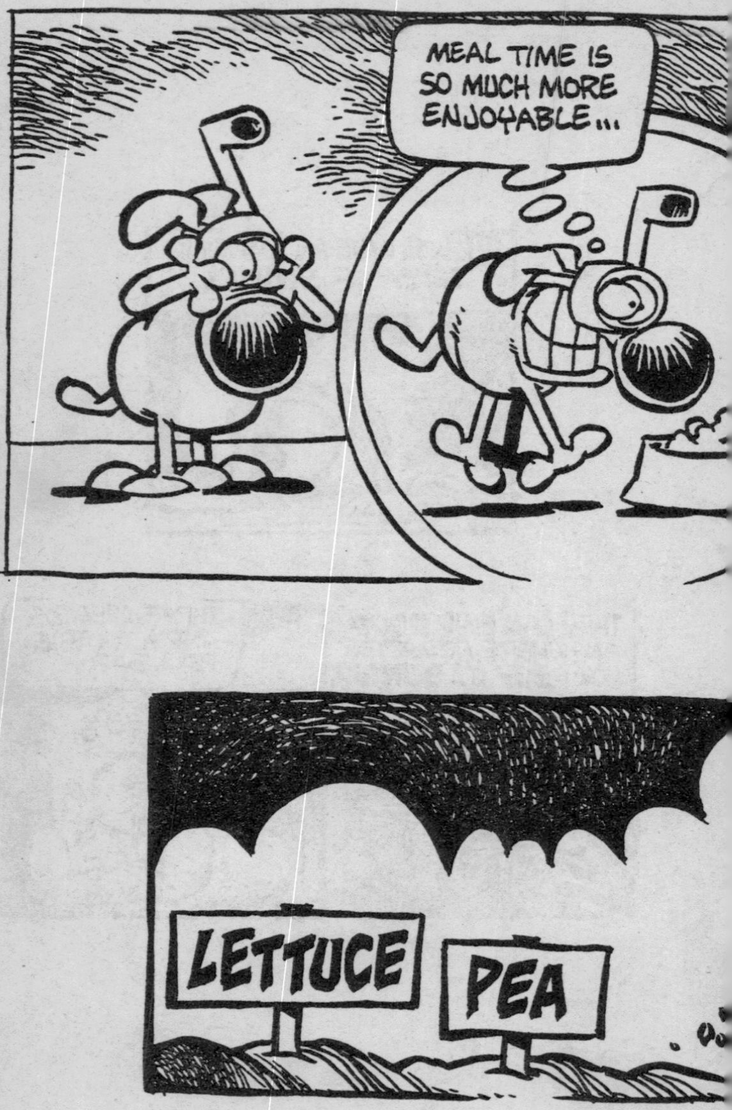
MEAL TIME IS SO MUCH MORE ENJOYABLE...
LETTUCE
PEA

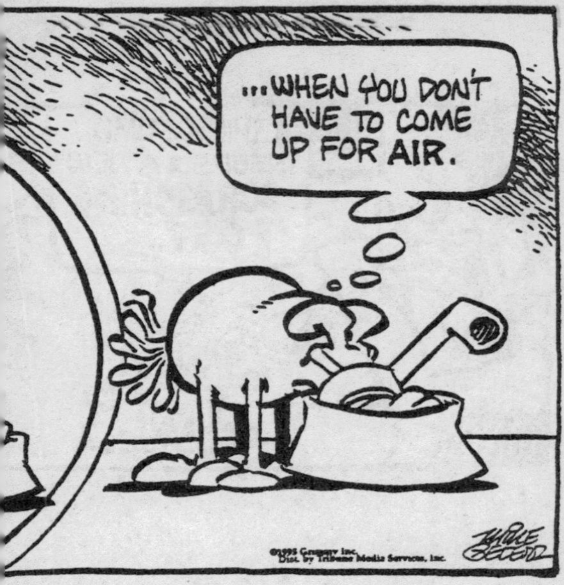
...WHEN YOU DON'T HAVE TO COME UP FOR AIR.
©1995 Grimmy Inc.
Dist. by Tribune Media Services, Inc.

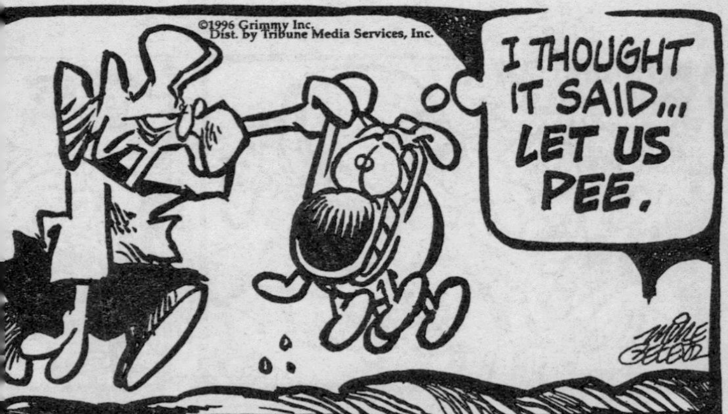
©1996 Grimmy Inc.
Dist. by Tribune Media Services, Inc.
I THOUGHT IT SAID... LET US PEE.

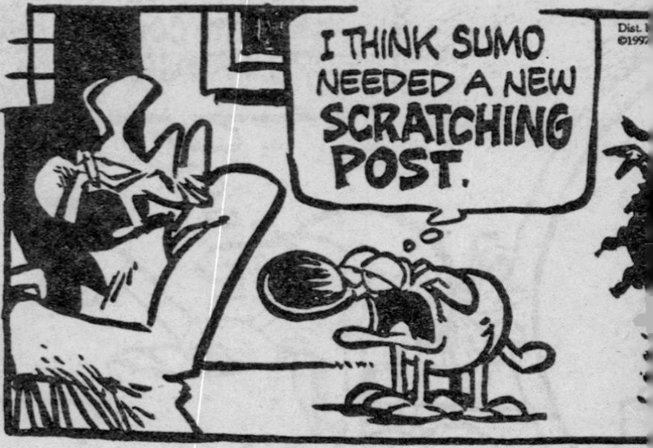
I THINK SUMO NEEDED A NEW SCRATCHING POST.

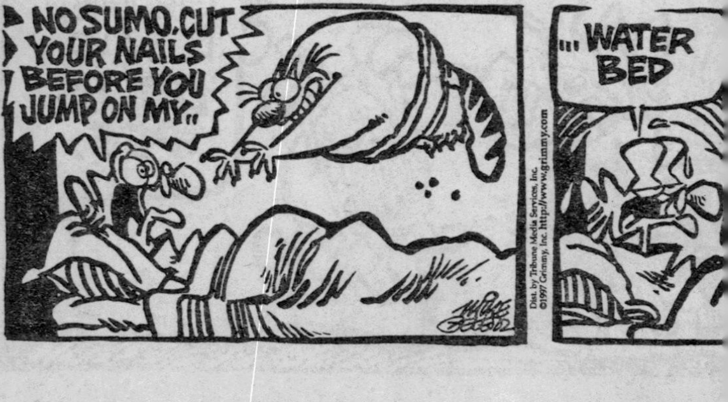
NO SUMO. CUT YOUR NAILS BEFORE YOU JUMP ON MY..
Dist. by Tribune Media Services, Inc.
©1997 Grimmy, Inc. http://www.grimmy.com
...WATER BED

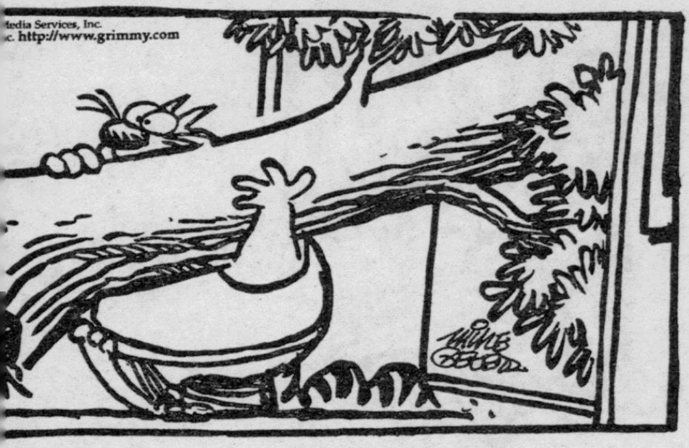
Media Services, Inc
c. http://www.grimmy.com

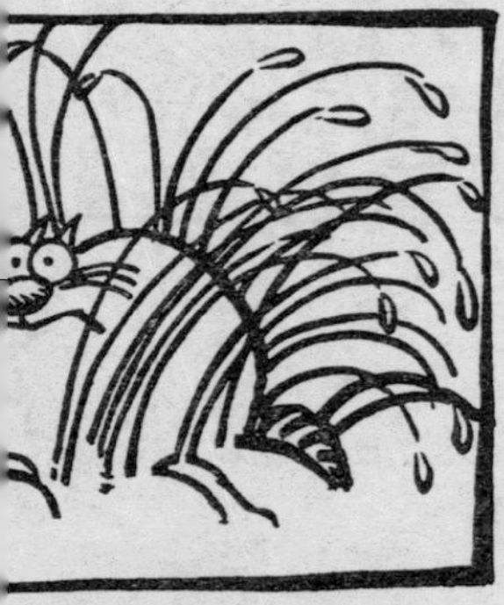

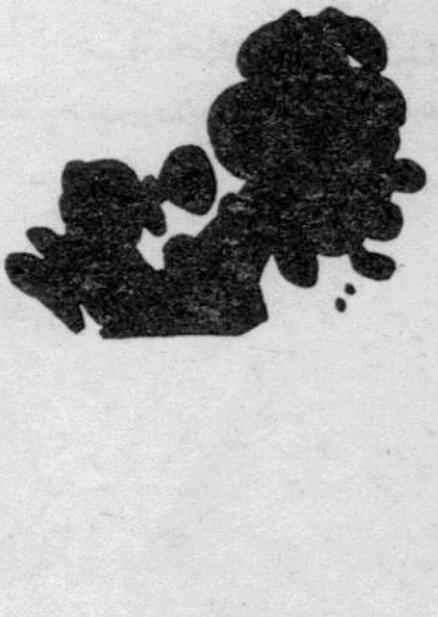

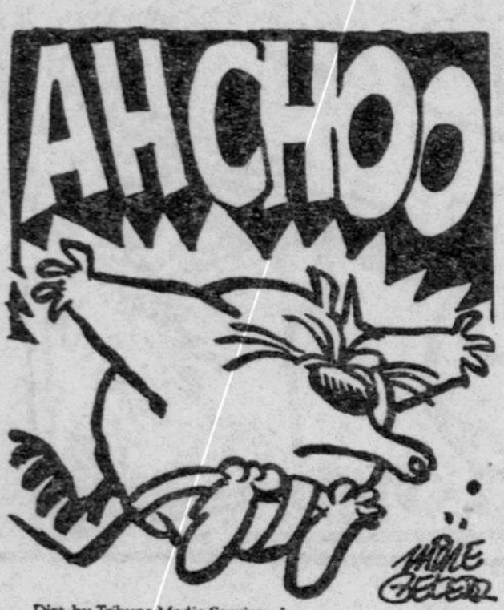
AHCHOO

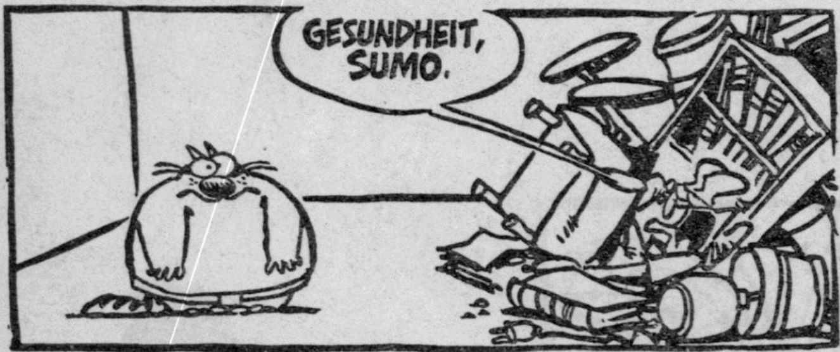
GESUNDHEIT, SUMO.

SUMO, THERE'S ONE SURE-FIRE WAY TO TELL IF A CAT IS OVERWEIGHT. TRY BACKING UP...
BEEP BEEP BEEP BEEP
NOW THAT'S OVER WEIGHT.
Dist. by Tribune Media Services, Inc. ©1997 Grimmy, Inc. http://www.grimmy.com

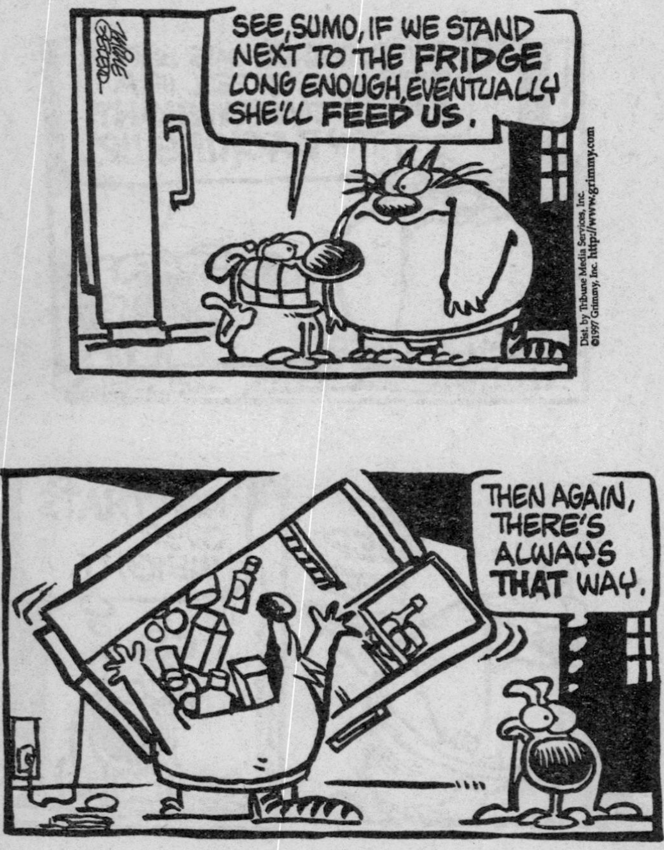
SEE, SUMO, IF WE STAND NEXT TO THE FRIDGE LONG ENOUGH, EVENTUALLY SHE'LL FEED US.
THEN AGAIN, THERE'S ALWAYS THAT WAY.

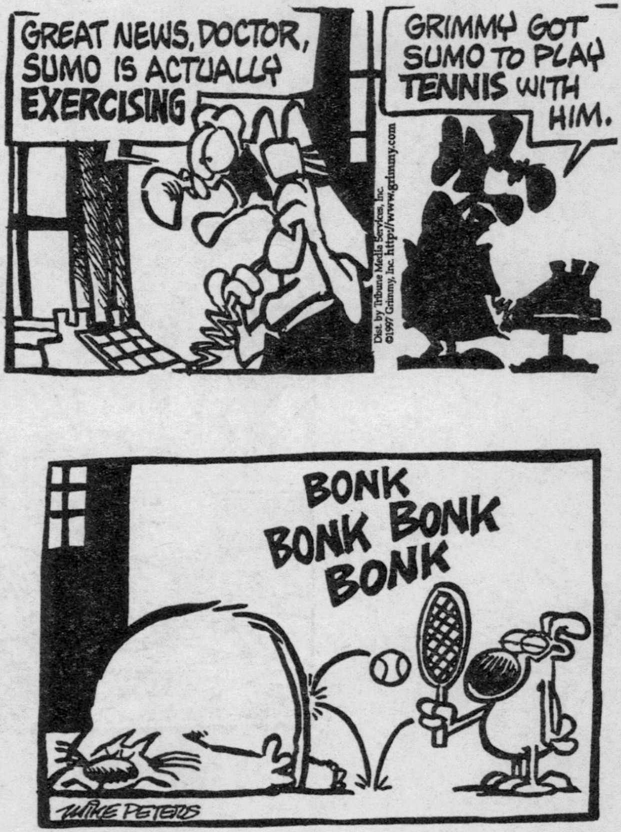
GREAT NEWS, DOCTOR, SUMO IS ACTUALLY EXERCISING
Dist. by Tribune Media Services, Inc.
©1997 Grimmy, Inc. http://www.grimmy.com
GRIMMY GOT SUMO TO PLAY TENNIS WITH HIM.
BONK
BONK BONK
BONK
MIKE PETERS

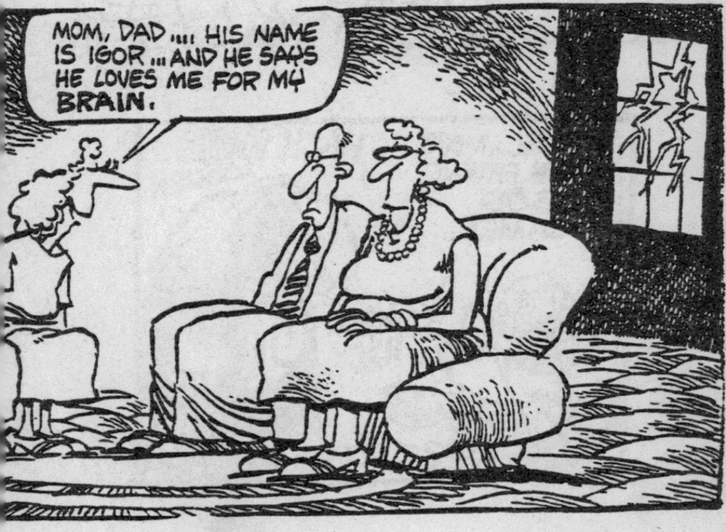
MOM, DAD.... HIS NAME IS IGOR... AND HE SAYS HE LOVES ME FOR MY BRAIN.

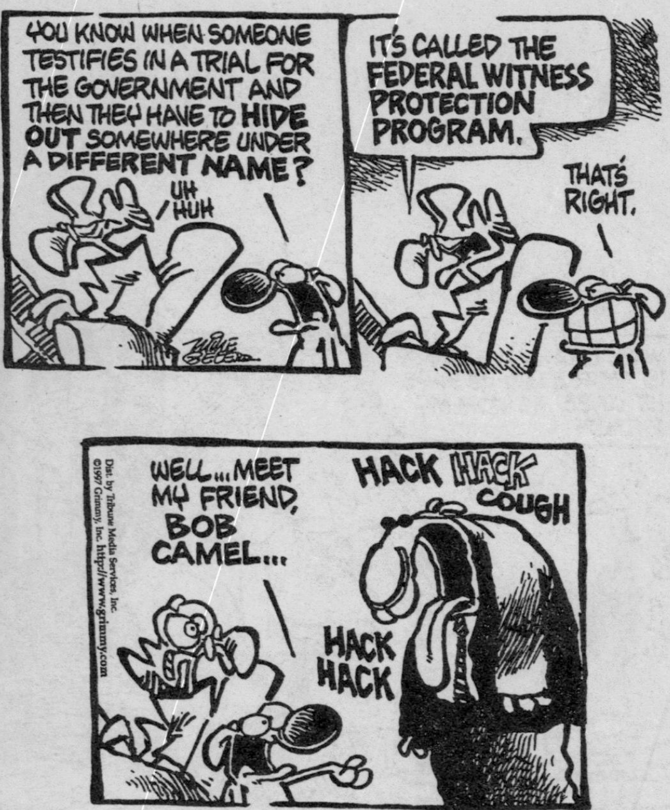
YOU KNOW WHEN SOMEONE TESTIFIES IN A TRIAL FOR THE GOVERNMENT AND THEN THEY HAVE TO HIDE OUT SOMEWHERE UNDER A DIFFERENT NAME?
UH HUH
IT'S CALLED THE FEDERAL WITNESS PROTECTION PROGRAM.
THAT'S RIGHT.
WELL... MEET MY FRIEND, BOB CAMEL...
HACK HACK
COUGH
HACK HACK
Dist. by Tribune Media Services, Inc.
©1997 Grimmy, Inc. http://www.grimmy.com

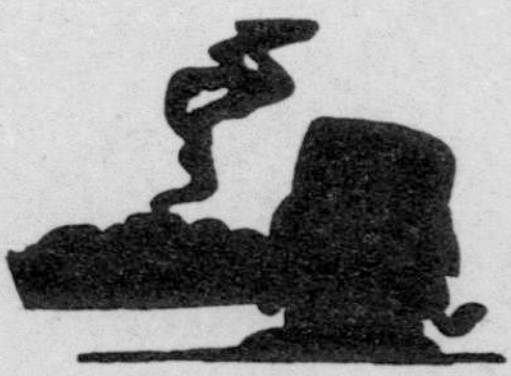

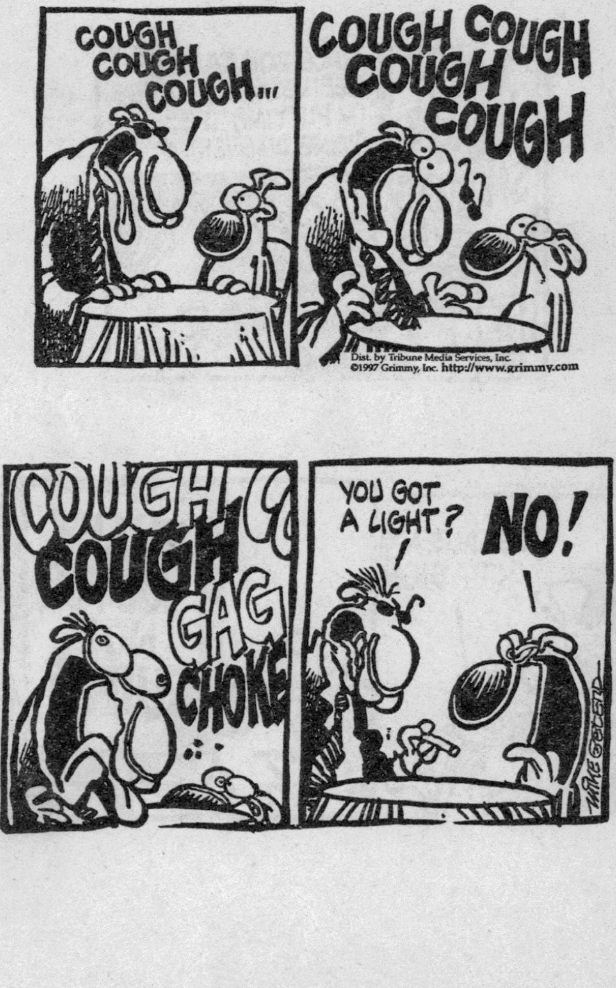
COUGH
COUGH
COUGH...
COUGH COUGH
COUGH
COUGH
Dist. by Tribune Media Services, Inc.
©1997 Grimmy, Inc. http://www.grimmy.com
COUGH
COUGH
GAG
CHOKE
YOU GOT A LIGHT?
NO!

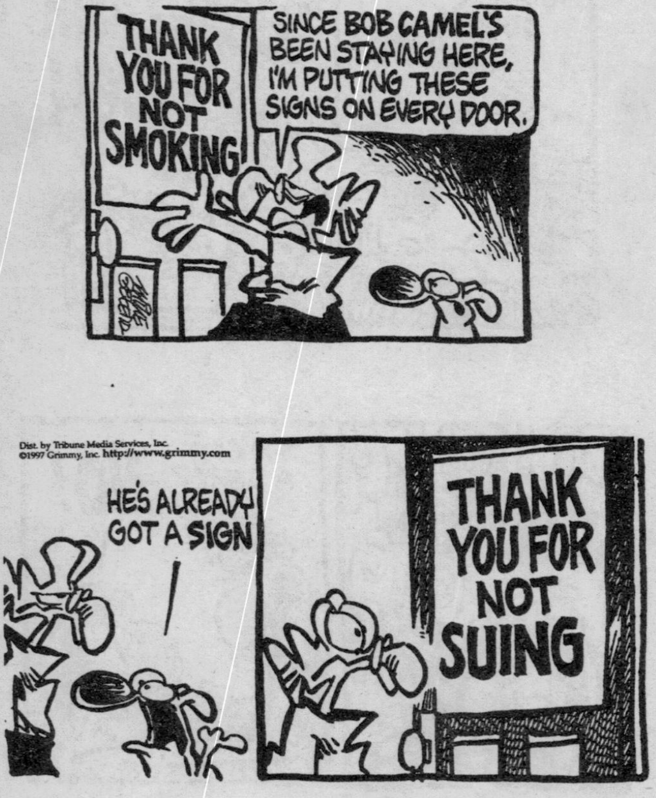
THANK YOU FOR NOT SMOKING
SINCE BOB CAMEL'S BEEN STAYING HERE, I'M PUTTING THESE SIGNS ON EVERY DOOR.
Dist. by Tribune Media Services, Inc.
©1997 Grimmy, Inc. http://www.grimmy.com
HE'S ALREADY GOT A SIGN
THANK YOU FOR NOT SUING

Dist. by Tribune Media Services, Inc.
©1997 Grimmy, Inc. http://www.grimmy.com
ISN'T THIS NICE SITTING HERE IN THE PARK, WATCHING CHILDREN PLAY?
PSST. HEY KID, SMOKE?
WHAT ARE YOU DOING? THESE ARE CHILDREN, THEY DON'T SMOKE CIGARETTES!
CHEW?
STOP THAT!!

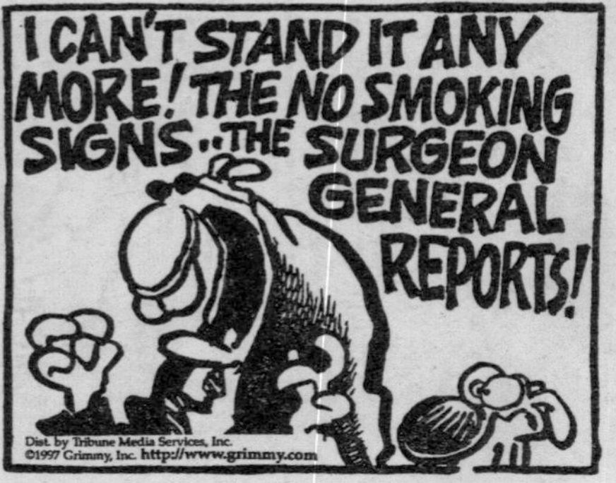
I CAN'T STAND IT ANY MORE! THE NO SMOKING SIGNS..THE SURGEON GENERAL REPORTS!
Dist. by Tribune Media Services, Inc.
©1997 Grimmy, Inc. http://www.grimmy.com

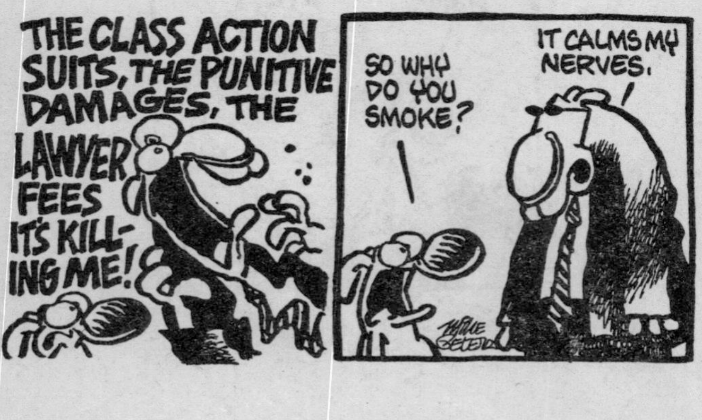
THE CLASS ACTION SUITS, THE PUNITIVE DAMAGES, THE LAWYER FEES IT'S KILLING ME!
SO WHY DO YOU SMOKE?
IT CALMS MY NERVES.

GRIMM, I DON'T WANT BOB CAMEL HIDING OUT IN THIS HOUSE. HE SMOKES TOO MUCH!
NO HE DOESN'T. HE QUIT SMOKING.
Dist. by Tribune Media Services, Inc. ©1997 Grimmy, Inc. http://www.grimmy.com
DIDN'T YOU BOB, DIDN'T YOU QUIT SMOKING?
COUGH...
I THINK THAT'S ONE COUGH FOR "YES" AND TWO COUGHS FOR "NO"

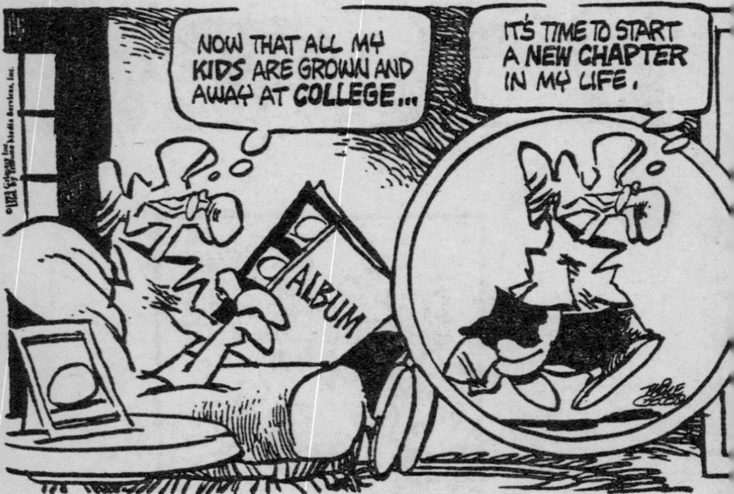
NOW THAT ALL MY KIDS ARE GROWN AND AWAY AT COLLEGE...
ALBUM
IT'S TIME TO START A NEW CHAPTER IN MY LIFE.

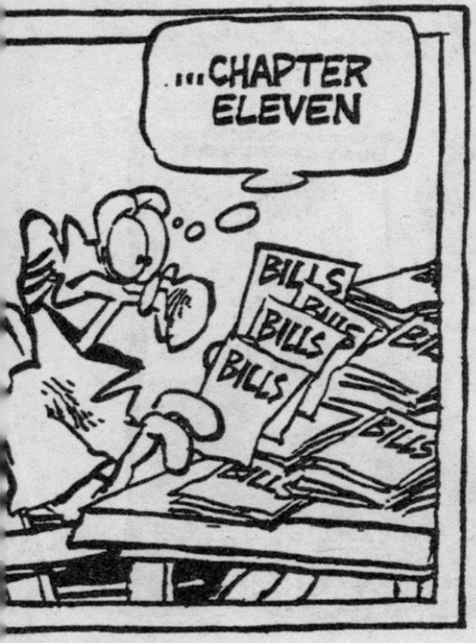
...CHAPTER ELEVEN
BILLS
BILLS
BILLS
BILLS

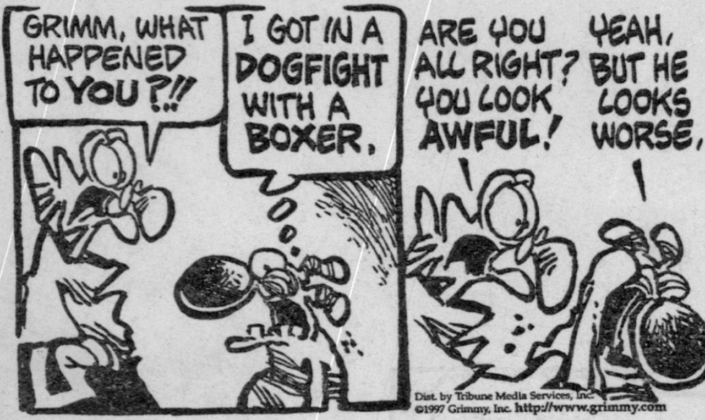
GRIMM, WHAT HAPPENED TO YOU?!!
I GOT IN A DOGFIGHT WITH A BOXER.
ARE YOU ALL RIGHT? YOU LOOK AWFUL!
YEAH, BUT HE LOOKS WORSE.
Dist. by Tribune Media Services, Inc.
©1997 Grimmy, Inc. http://www.grimmy.com

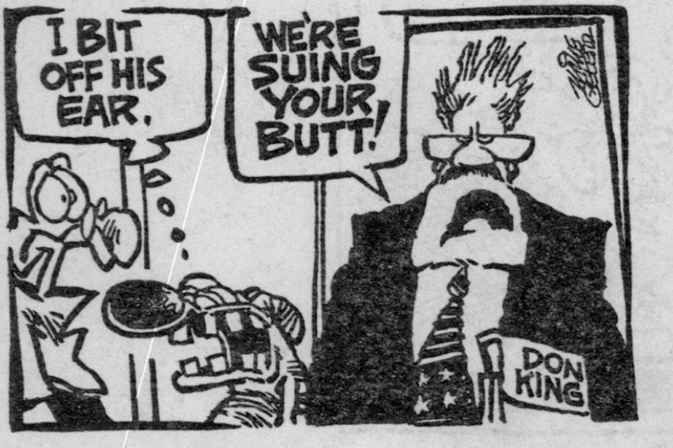
I BIT OFF HIS EAR.
WE'RE SUING YOUR BUTT!
DON KING

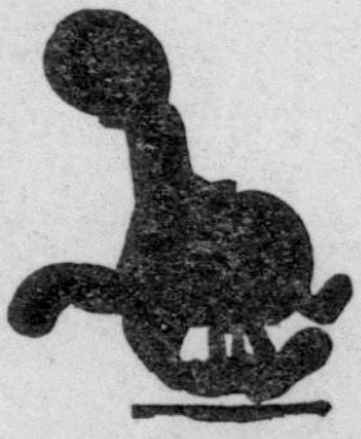

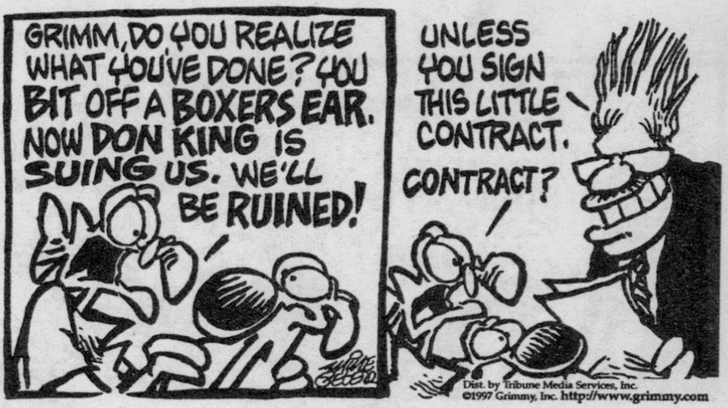
GRIMM, DO YOU REALIZE WHAT YOU'VE DONE? YOU BIT OFF A BOXERS EAR. NOW DON KING IS SUING US. WE'LL BE RUINED!
UNLESS YOU SIGN THIS LITTLE CONTRACT.
CONTRACT?
Dist. by Tribune Media Services, Inc.
©1997 Grimmy, Inc. http://www.grimmy.com

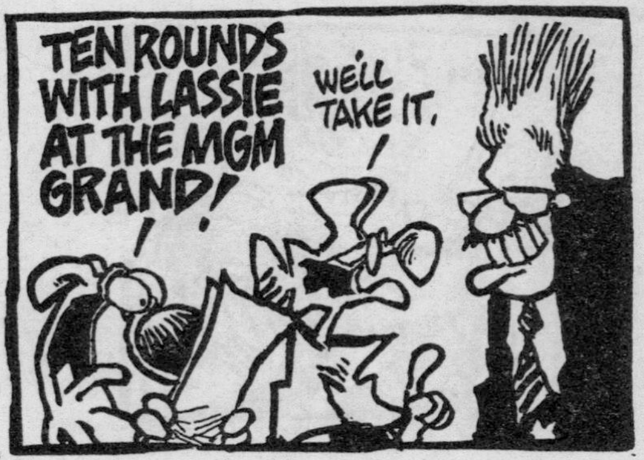
TEN ROUNDS WITH LASSIE AT THE MGM GRAND!
WE'LL TAKE IT.

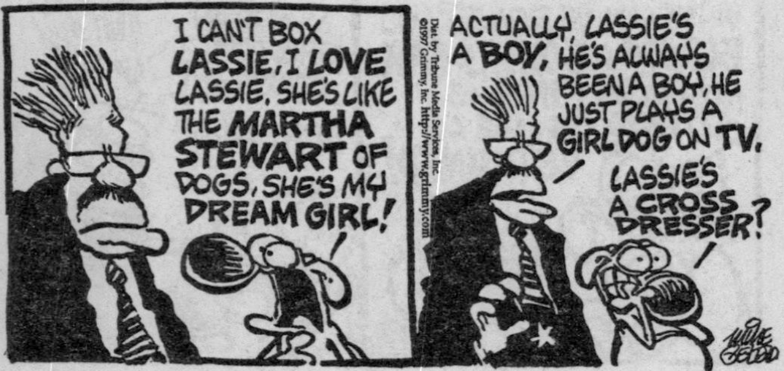
I CAN'T BOX LASSIE, I LOVE LASSIE. SHE'S LIKE THE MARTHA STEWART OF DOGS, SHE'S MY DREAM GIRL!
Dist. by Tribune Media Services, Inc. ©1997 Grimmy, Inc. http://www.grimmy.com
ACTUALLY, LASSIE'S A BOY, HE'S ALWAYS BEEN A BOY, HE JUST PLAYS A GIRL DOG ON TV.
LASSIE'S A CROSS DRESSER?

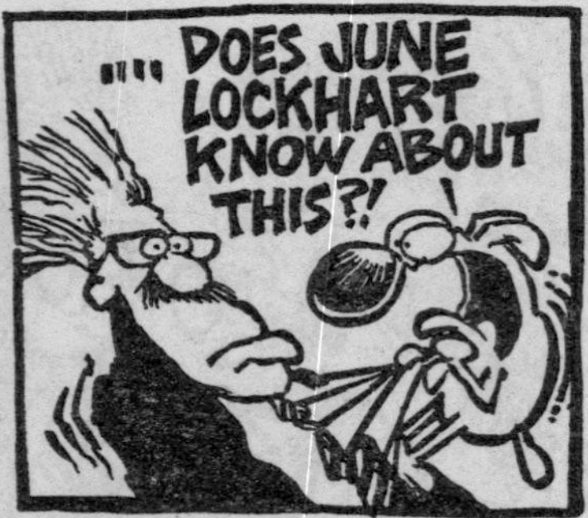
"... DOES JUNE LOCKHART KNOW ABOUT THIS?!

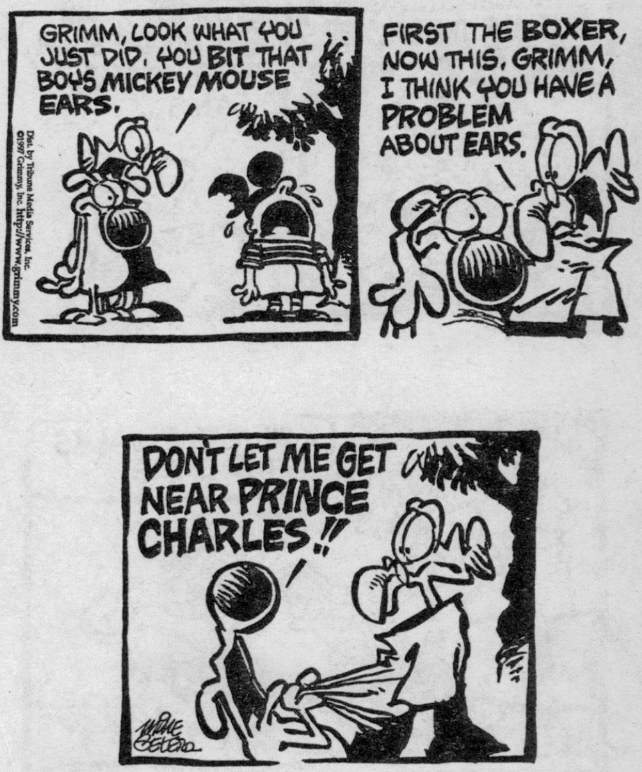
GRIMM, LOOK WHAT YOU JUST DID. YOU BIT THAT BOYS MICKEY MOUSE EARS.
Dist. by Tribune Media Services, Inc. ©1997 Grimmy, Inc. http://www.grimmy.com
FIRST THE BOXER, NOW THIS. GRIMM, I THINK YOU HAVE A PROBLEM ABOUT EARS.
DON'T LET ME GET NEAR PRINCE CHARLES!!

SO HOW HAVE THINGS CHANGED SINCE GRIMM BIT OFF THE BOXERS EAR?
OH, NOTHING'S CHANGED, WE GET UP THE SAME, WE EAT THE SAME...
Dist. by Tribune Media Services, Inc.
©1997 Grimmy, Inc. http://www.grimmy.com

...WE TAKE WALKS THE SAME.

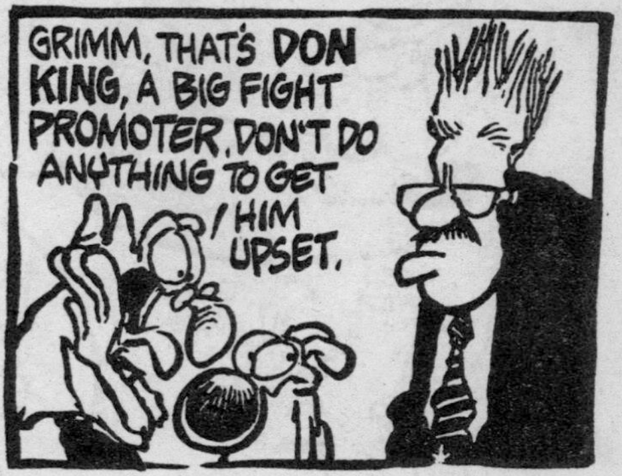
GRIMM, THAT'S **DON KING**, A BIG FIGHT PROMOTER. DON'T DO ANYTHING TO GET HIM UPSET.

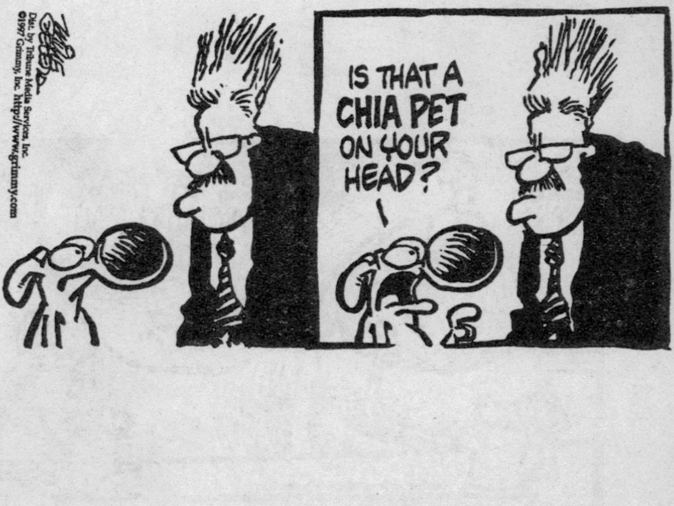
Dist. by Tribune Media Services, Inc.
©1997 Grimmy, Inc. http://www.grimmy.com
IS THAT A **CHIA PET** ON YOUR HEAD?

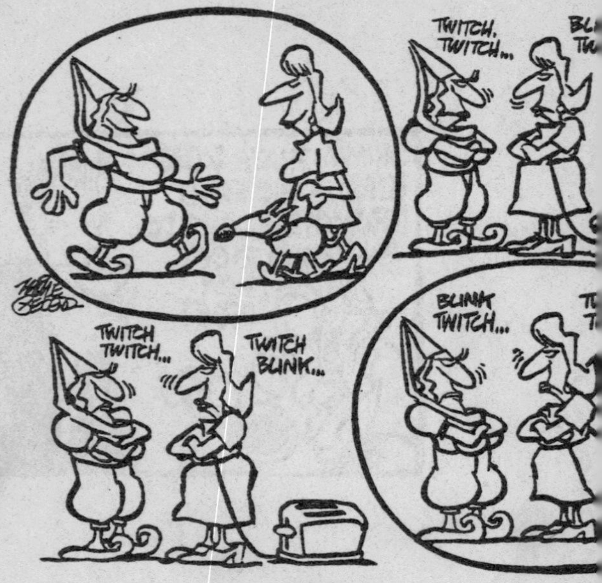
TWITCH, TWITCH...
TWITCH TWITCH...
TWITCH BLINK...
BLINK TWITCH...

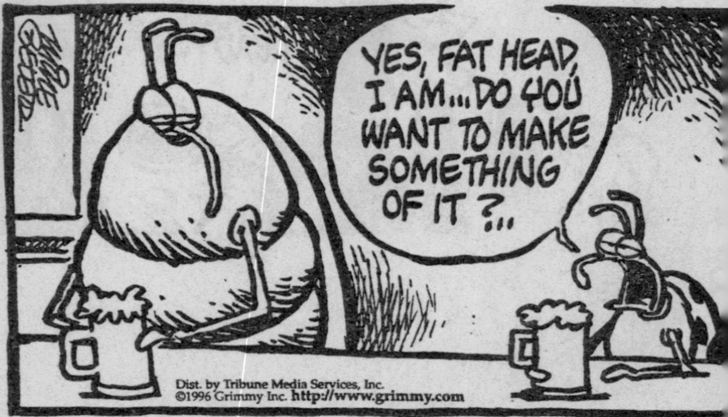
YES, FAT HEAD, I AM... DO YOU WANT TO MAKE SOMETHING OF IT ?...
Dist. by Tribune Media Services, Inc.
©1996 Grimmy Inc. http://www.grimmy.com

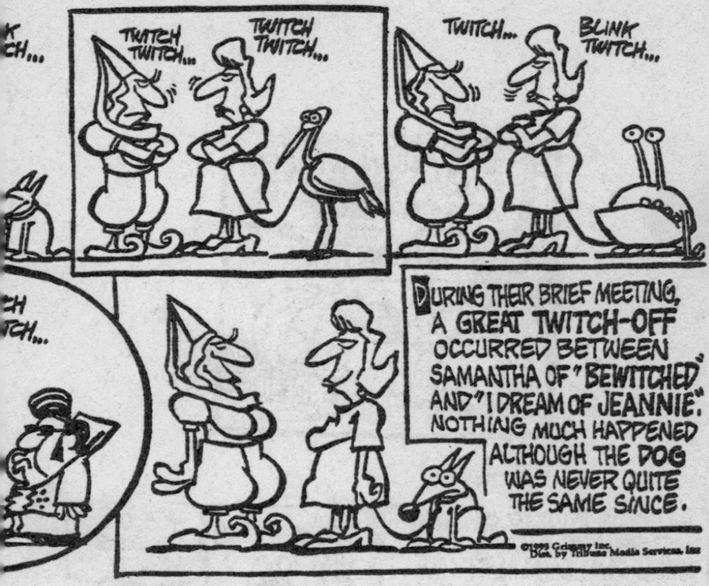
TWITCH TWITCH...
TWITCH TWITCH...
TWITCH...
BLINK TWITCH...
DURING THEIR BRIEF MEETING, A GREAT TWITCH-OFF OCCURRED BETWEEN SAMANTHA OF "BEWITCHED" AND "I DREAM OF JEANNIE". NOTHING MUCH HAPPENED ALTHOUGH THE DOG WAS NEVER QUITE THE SAME SINCE.

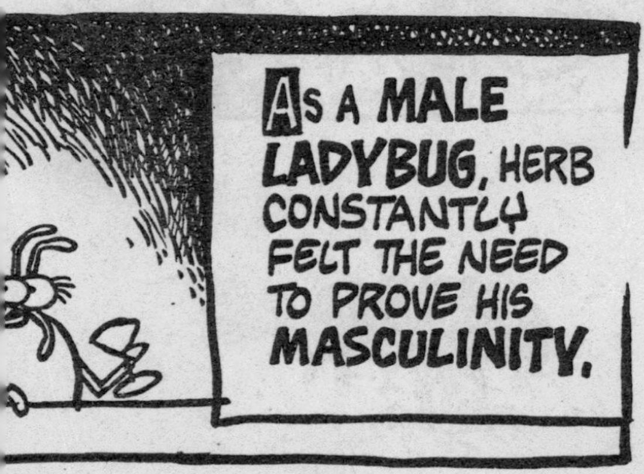
AS A MALE LADYBUG, HERB CONSTANTLY FELT THE NEED TO PROVE HIS MASCULINITY.

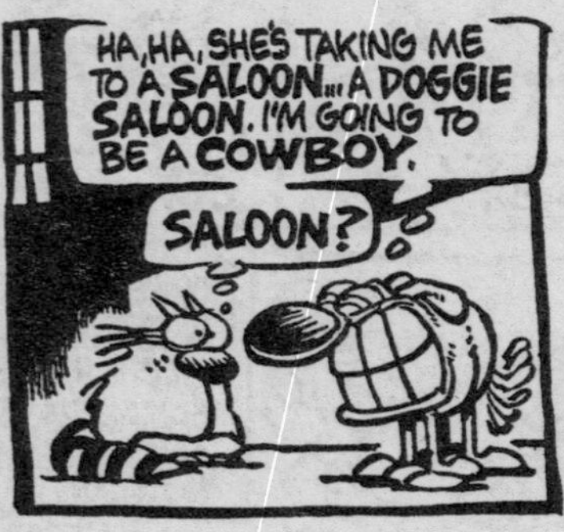
HA, HA, SHE'S TAKING ME TO A SALOON... A DOGGIE SALOON. I'M GOING TO BE A COWBOY.
SALOON?

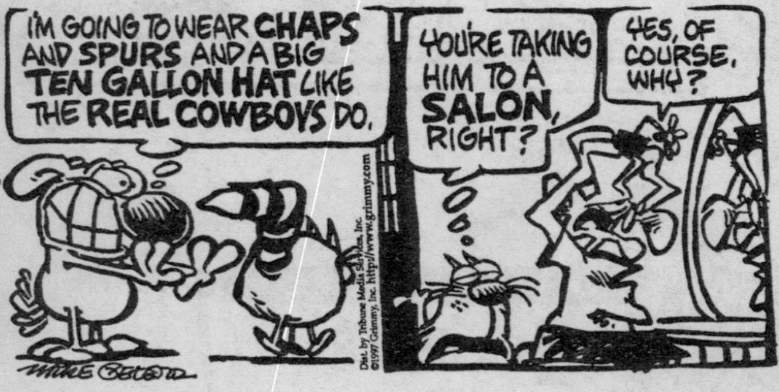
I'M GOING TO WEAR CHAPS AND SPURS AND A BIG TEN GALLON HAT LIKE THE REAL COWBOYS DO.
Dist. by Tribune Media Services, Inc. ©1997 Grimmy, Inc. http://www.grimmy.com
YOU'RE TAKING HIM TO A SALON, RIGHT?
YES, OF COURSE, WHY?

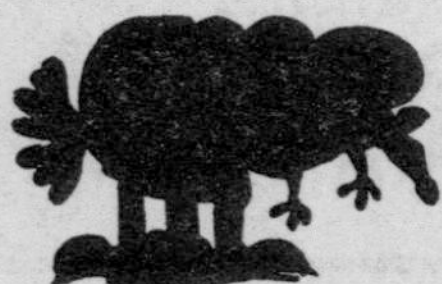

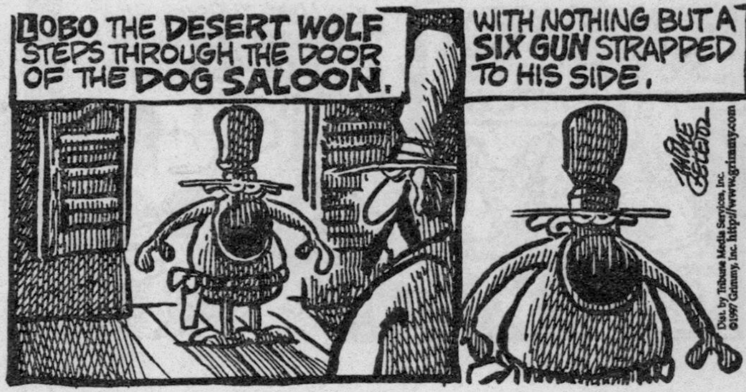
LOBO THE DESERT WOLF STEPS THROUGH THE DOOR OF THE DOG SALOON.
WITH NOTHING BUT A SIX GUN STRAPPED TO HIS SIDE.
Dist. by Tribune Media Services, Inc.
©1997 Grimmy, Inc. http://www.grimmy.com

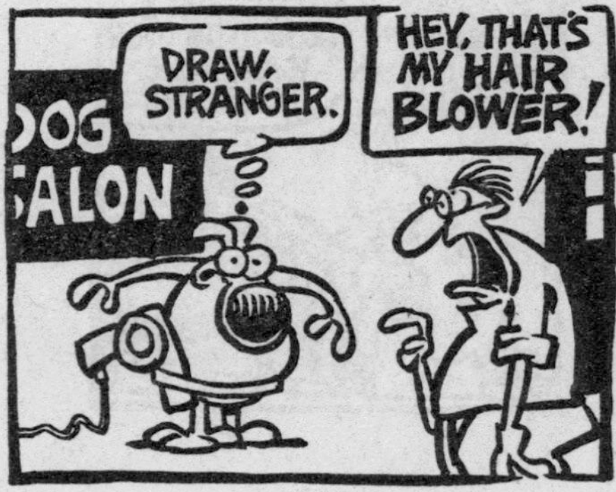
DRAW, STRANGER.
HEY, THAT'S MY HAIR BLOWER!
DOG SALON

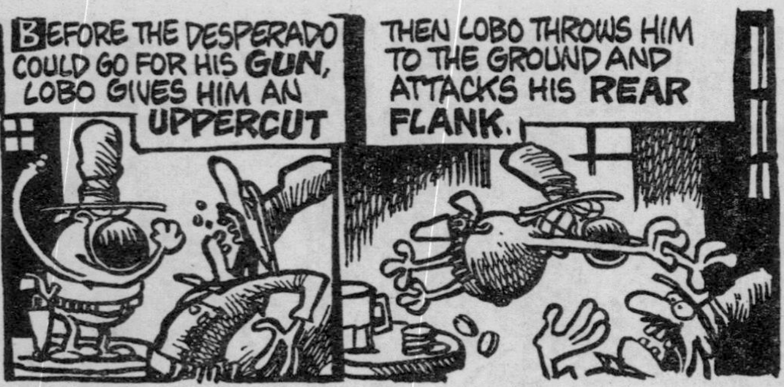
BEFORE THE DESPERADO COULD GO FOR HIS GUN, LOBO GIVES HIM AN UPPERCUT
THEN LOBO THROWS HIM TO THE GROUND AND ATTACKS HIS REAR FLANK.

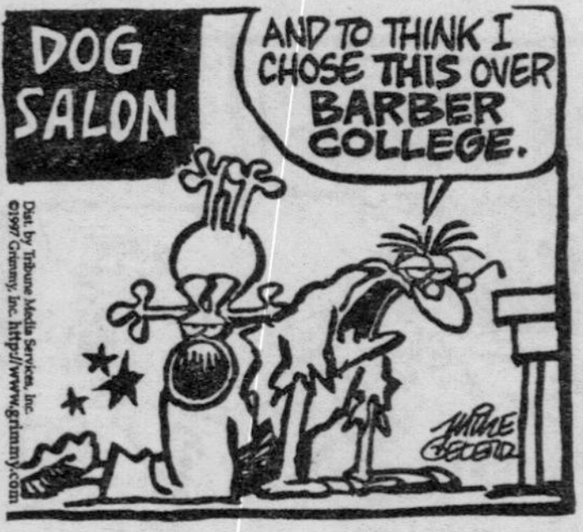
DOG SALON
AND TO THINK I CHOSE THIS OVER BARBER COLLEGE.
Dist. by Tribune Media Services, Inc.
©1997 Grimmy, Inc. http://www.grimmy.com

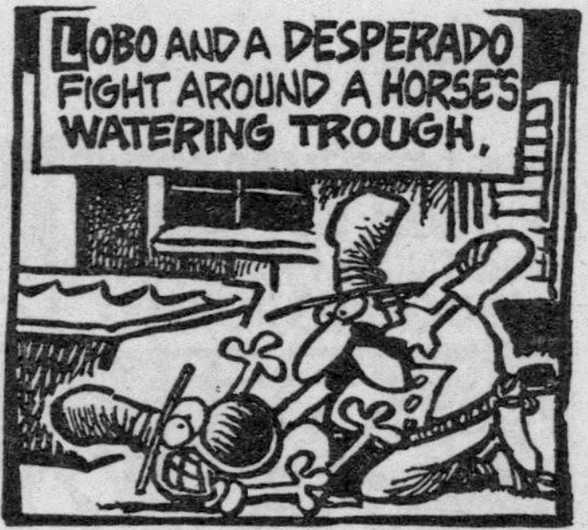
LOBO AND A DESPERADO FIGHT AROUND A HORSE'S WATERING TROUGH.

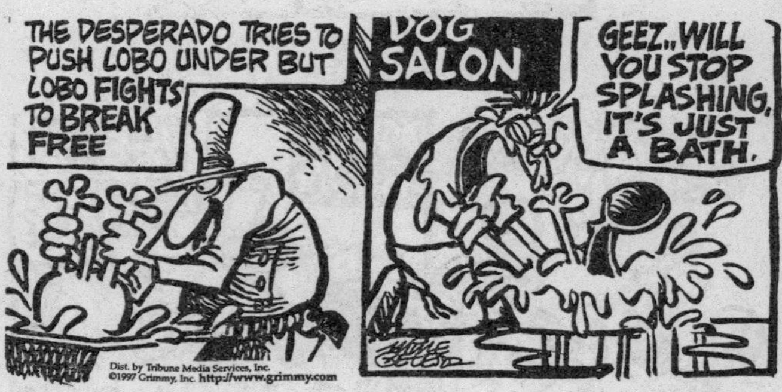
THE DESPERADO TRIES TO PUSH LOBO UNDER BUT LOBO FIGHTS TO BREAK FREE
DOG SALON
GEEZ.. WILL YOU STOP SPLASHING. IT'S JUST A BATH.
Dist. by Tribune Media Services, Inc.
©1997 Grimmy, Inc. http://www.grimmy.com

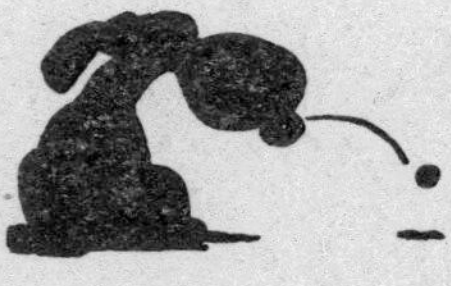

THE DESPERADO DRAWS HIS GUN, BUT WITH LIGHTNING FAST SPEED LOBO GRABS HIS HAND.
FOR LOBO KNEW THE OUTLAW WANTED TO BLOW HIM AWAY.
DOG SALON
WILL SOMEBODY HELP ME DRY OFF THIS DOG?
Dist. by Tribune Media Services, Inc.
©1997 Grimmy, Inc. http://www.grimmy.com

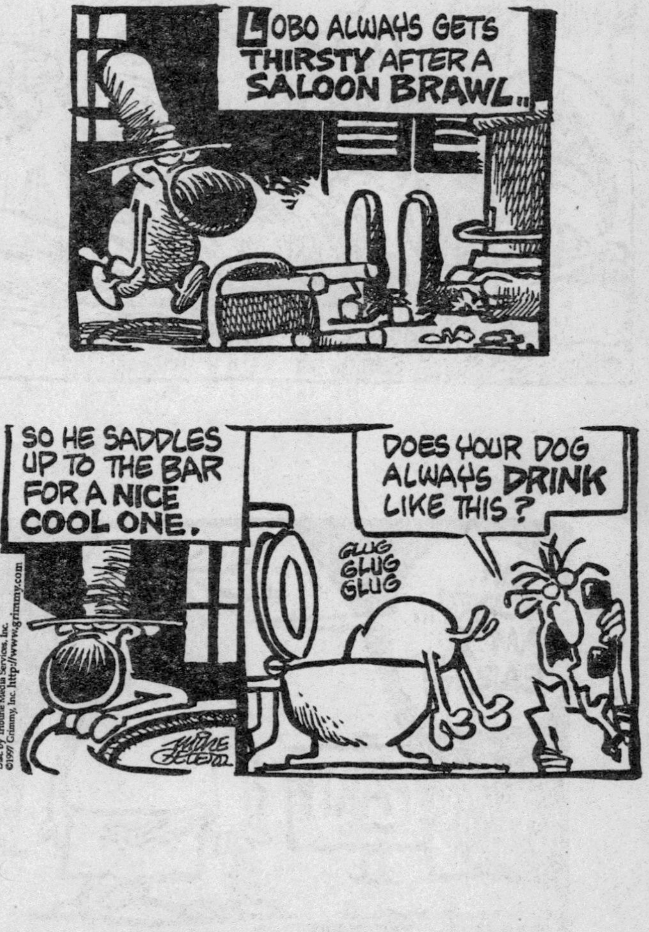
LOBO ALWAYS GETS THIRSTY AFTER A SALOON BRAWL..
SO HE SADDLES UP TO THE BAR FOR A NICE COOL ONE.
DOES YOUR DOG ALWAYS DRINK LIKE THIS?
GLUG GLUG GLUG

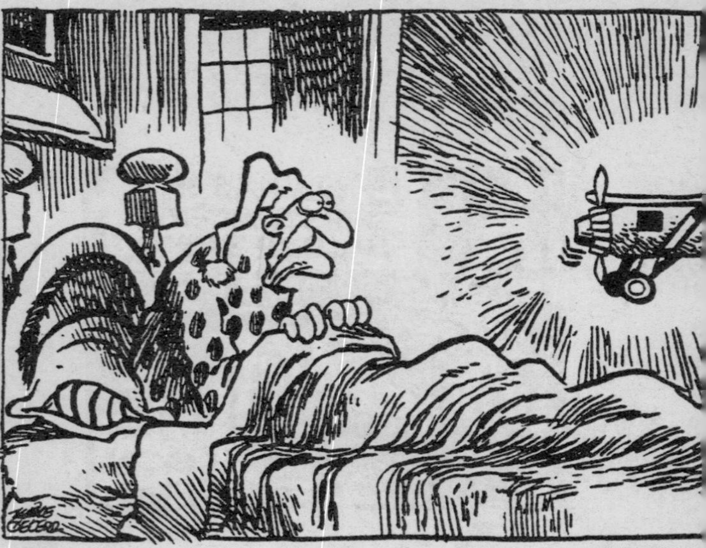

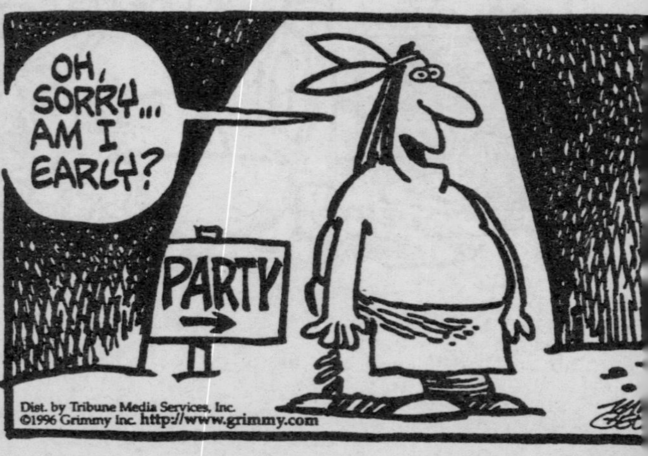
OH, SORRY... AM I EARLY?
PARTY
Dist. by Tribune Media Services, Inc.
©1996 Grimmy Inc. http://www.grimmy.com

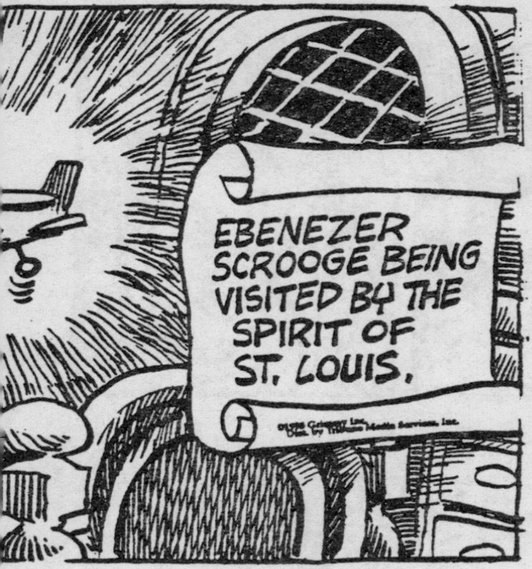
EBENEZER SCROOGE BEING VISITED BY THE SPIRIT OF ST. LOUIS.

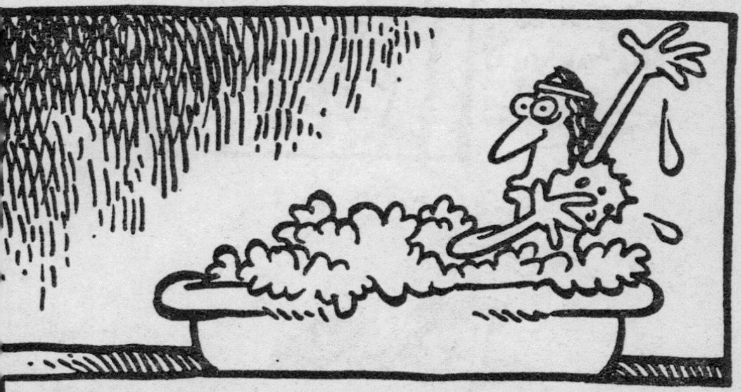

THE FIRST OF THE MOHICANS

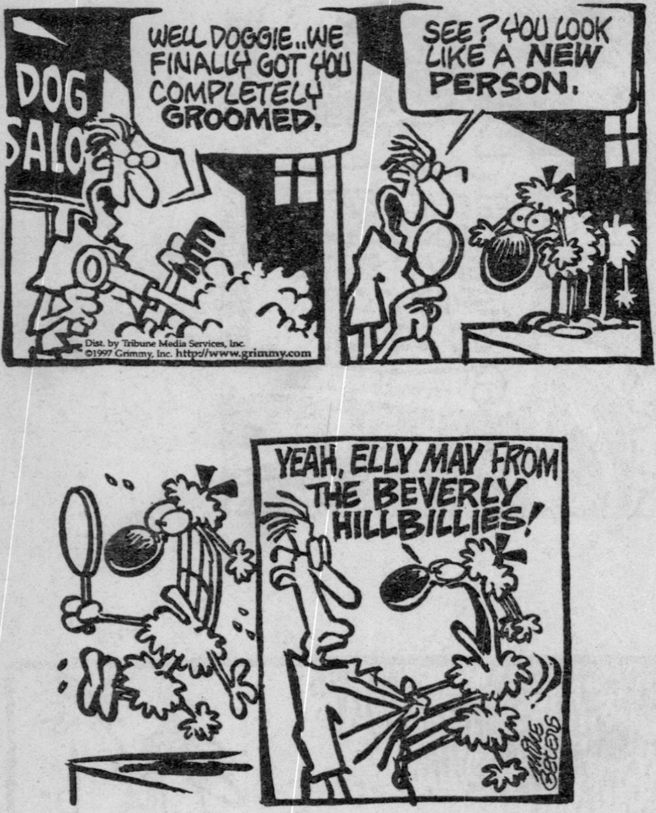
DOG
SALO
WELL DOGGIE..WE FINALLY GOT YOU COMPLETELY GROOMED.
Dist. by Tribune Media Services, Inc.
©1997 Grimmy, Inc. http://www.grimmy.com
SEE? YOU LOOK LIKE A NEW PERSON.
YEAH, ELLY MAY FROM THE BEVERLY HILLBILLIES!

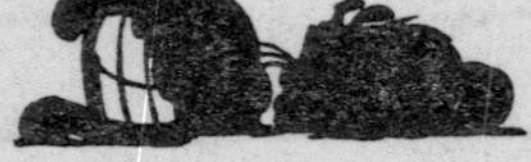

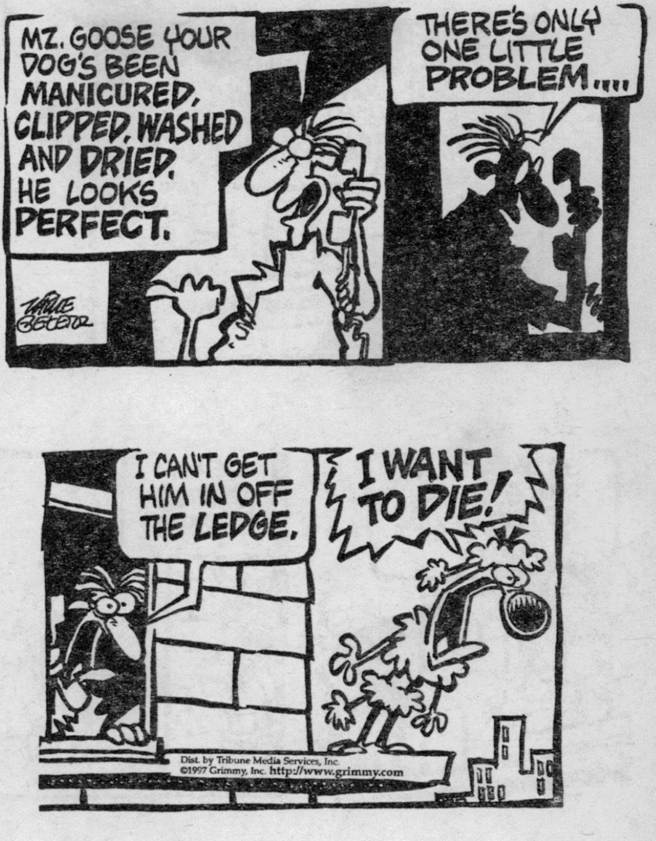

MZ. GOOSE YOUR DOG'S BEEN MANICURED, CLIPPED, WASHED AND DRIED. HE LOOKS PERFECT.
THERE'S ONLY ONE LITTLE PROBLEM.....
I CAN'T GET HIM IN OFF THE LEDGE.
I WANT TO DIE!
Dist. by Tribune Media Services, Inc.
©1997 Grimmy, Inc. http://www.grimmy.com

PLEASE COME INSIDE, GRIMM, YOU DON'T LOOK LIKE A GIRL YOU LOOK LIKE A GUY, REALLY.
Dist. by Tribune Media Services, Inc.
©1997 Grimmy, Inc. http://www.grimmy.com

GO ON, ATTILA, TELL GRIMMY HE LOOKS LIKE A GUY.
YEAH, DENNIS RODMAN

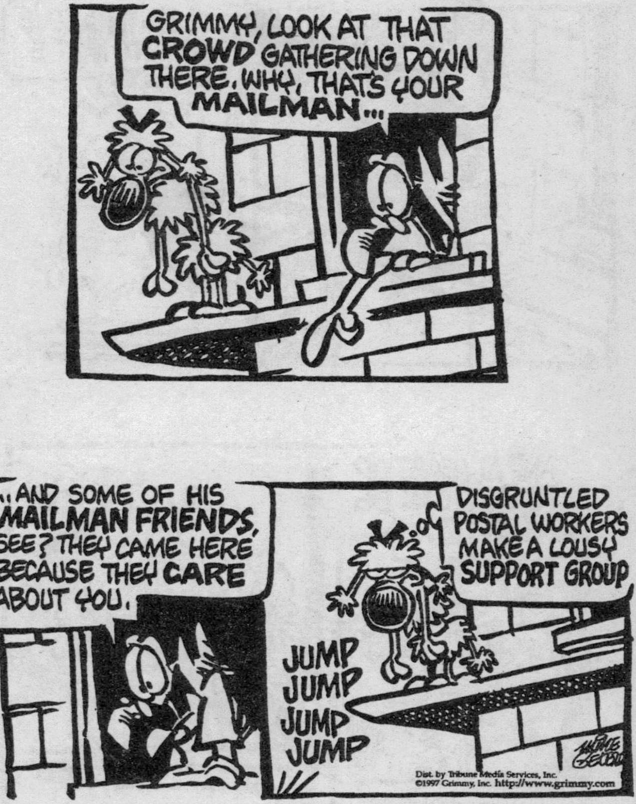
GRIMMY, LOOK AT THAT CROWD GATHERING DOWN THERE. WHY, THAT'S YOUR MAILMAN...
...AND SOME OF HIS MAILMAN FRIENDS, SEE? THEY CAME HERE BECAUSE THEY CARE ABOUT YOU.
DISGRUNTLED POSTAL WORKERS MAKE A LOUSY SUPPORT GROUP
JUMP
JUMP
JUMP
JUMP
Dist. by Tribune Media Services, Inc.
©1997 Grimmy, Inc. http://www.grimmy.com

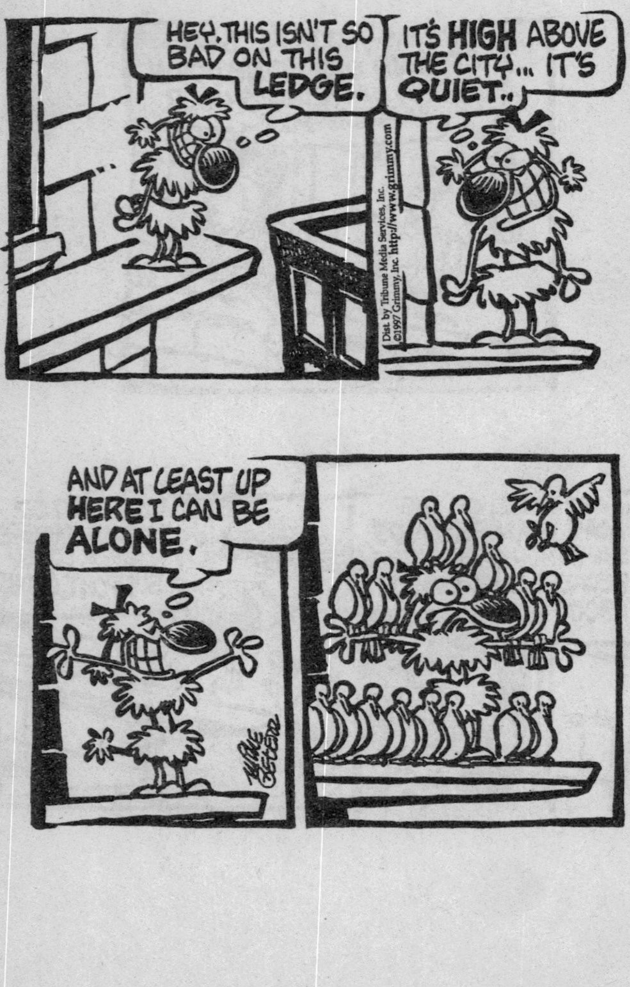
HEY. THIS ISN'T SO BAD ON THIS LEDGE.
IT'S HIGH ABOVE THE CITY... IT'S QUIET..
Dist. by Tribune Media Services, Inc. ©1997 Grimmy, Inc. http://www.grimmy.com
AND AT LEAST UP HERE I CAN BE ALONE.

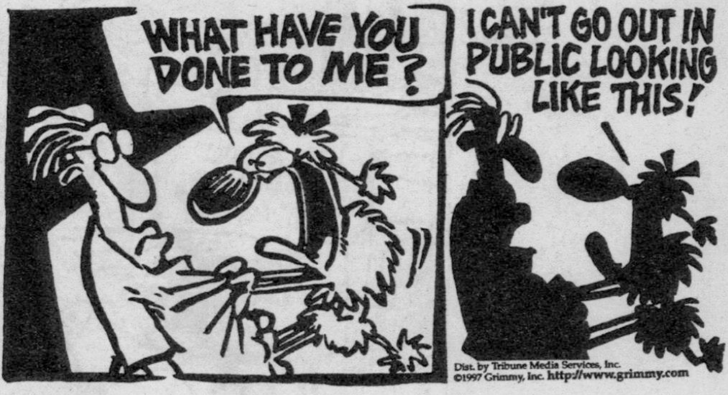
WHAT HAVE YOU DONE TO ME?
I CAN'T GO OUT IN PUBLIC LOOKING LIKE THIS!
Dist. by Tribune Media Services, Inc.
©1997 Grimmy, Inc. http://www.grimmy.com

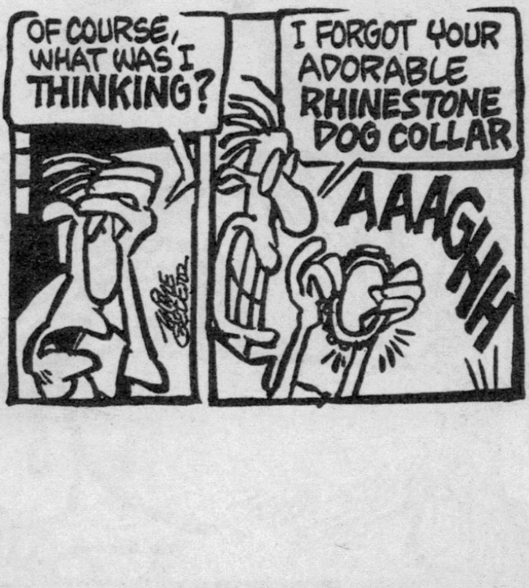
OF COURSE, WHAT WAS I THINKING?
I FORGOT YOUR ADORABLE RHINESTONE DOG COLLAR
AAAGHH

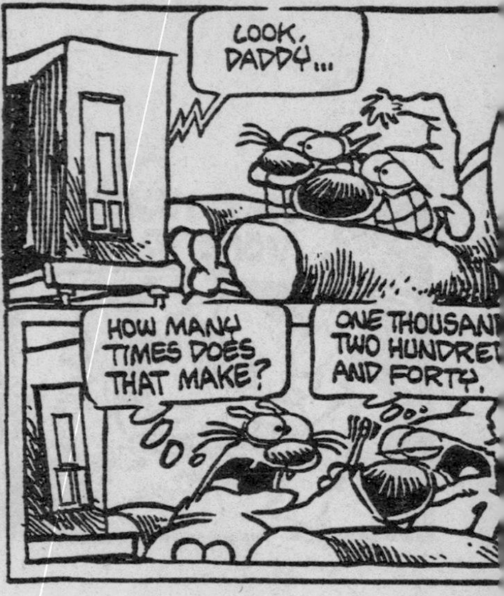
LOOK, DADDY...
HOW MANY TIMES DOES THAT MAKE?
ONE THOUSAN
TWO HUNDRE
AND FORTY.

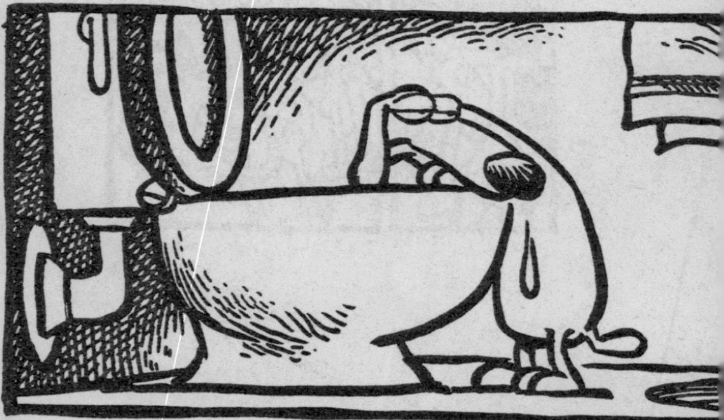

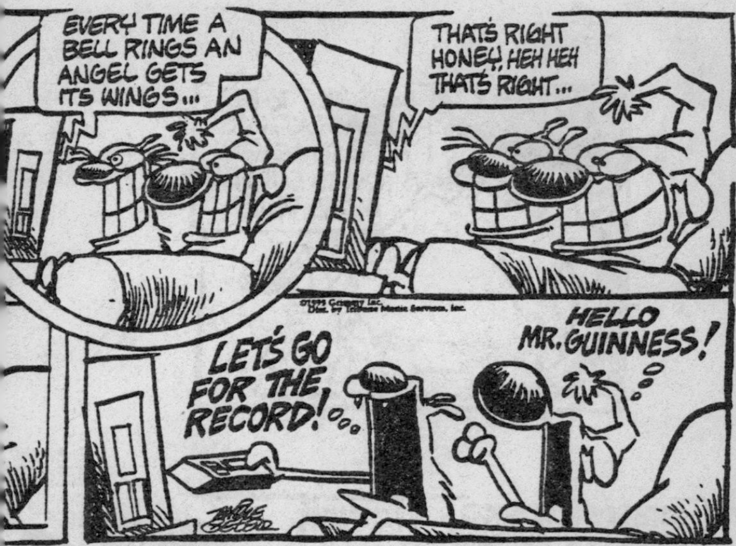
EVERY TIME A BELL RINGS AN ANGEL GETS ITS WINGS...
THAT'S RIGHT HONEY, HEH HEH THAT'S RIGHT...
LET'S GO FOR THE RECORD!
HELLO MR. GUINNESS!

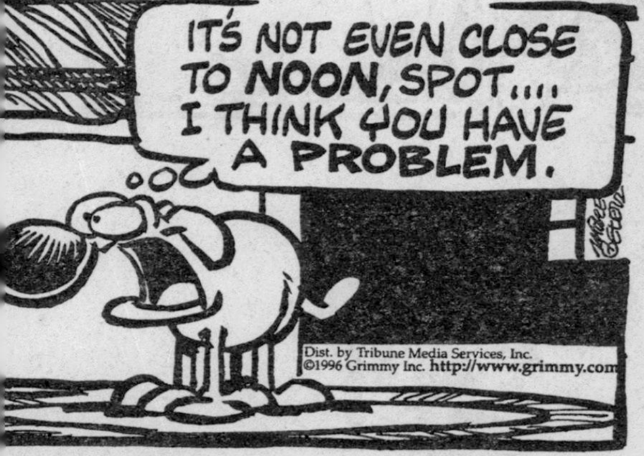
IT'S NOT EVEN CLOSE TO NOON, SPOT.... I THINK YOU HAVE A PROBLEM.
Dist. by Tribune Media Services, Inc.
©1996 Grimmy Inc. http://www.grimmy.com

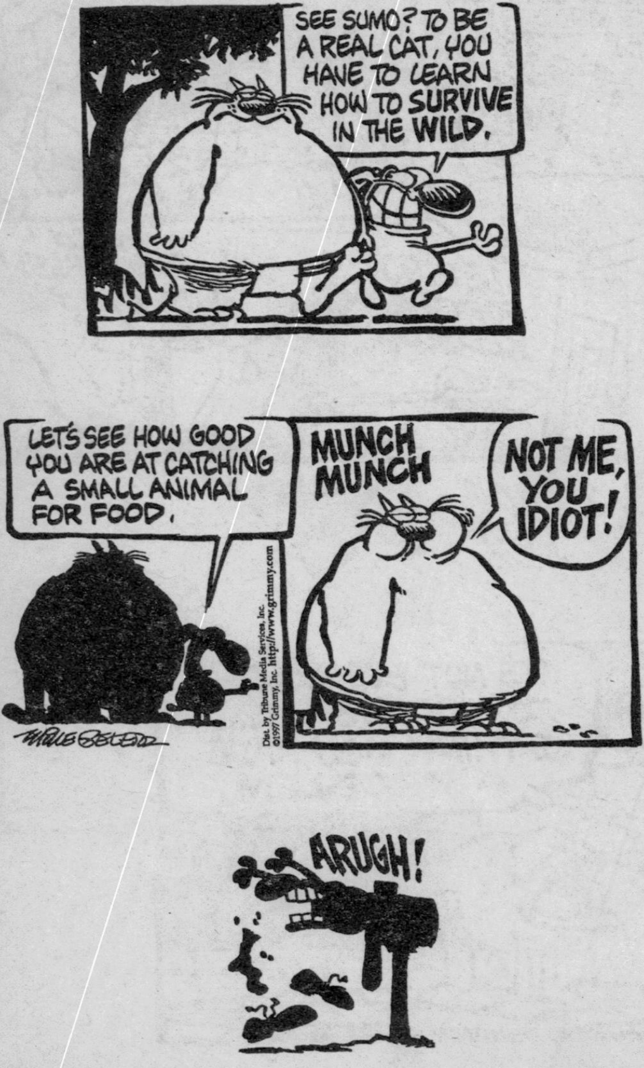
SEE SUMO? TO BE A REAL CAT, YOU HAVE TO LEARN HOW TO SURVIVE IN THE WILD.
LET'S SEE HOW GOOD YOU ARE AT CATCHING A SMALL ANIMAL FOR FOOD.
Dist. by Tribune Media Services, Inc. ©1997 Grimmy, Inc. http://www.grimmy.com
MUNCH MUNCH
NOT ME, YOU IDIOT!
ARUGH!

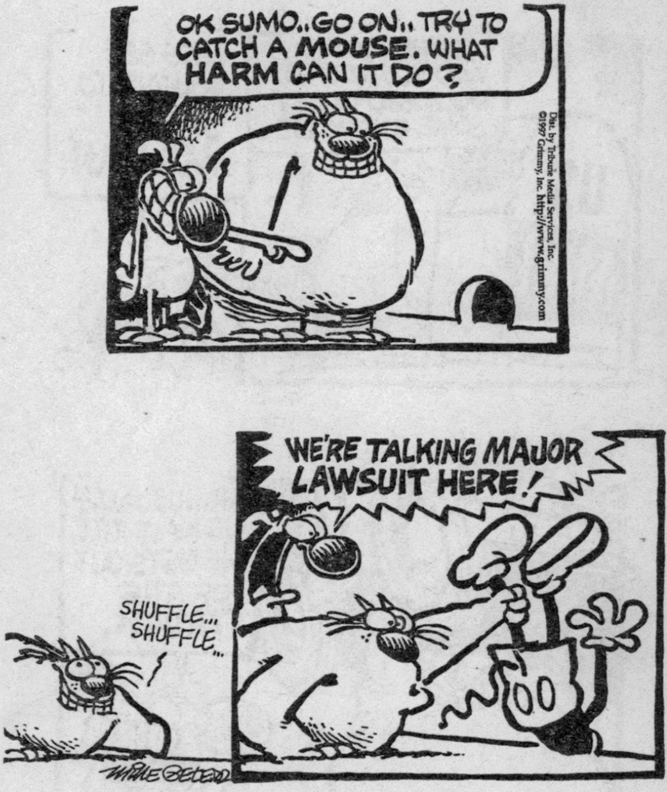
OK SUMO..GO ON.. TRY TO CATCH A MOUSE. WHAT HARM CAN IT DO?
Dist. by Tribune Media Services, Inc. ©1997 Grimmy, Inc. http://www.grimmy.com
WE'RE TALKING MAJOR LAWSUIT HERE!
SHUFFLE... SHUFFLE...

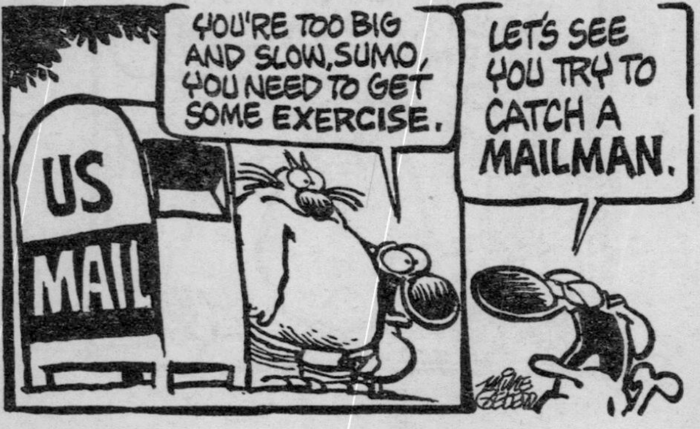
US MAIL
YOU'RE TOO BIG AND SLOW, SUMO, YOU NEED TO GET SOME EXERCISE.
LET'S SEE YOU TRY TO CATCH A MAILMAN.

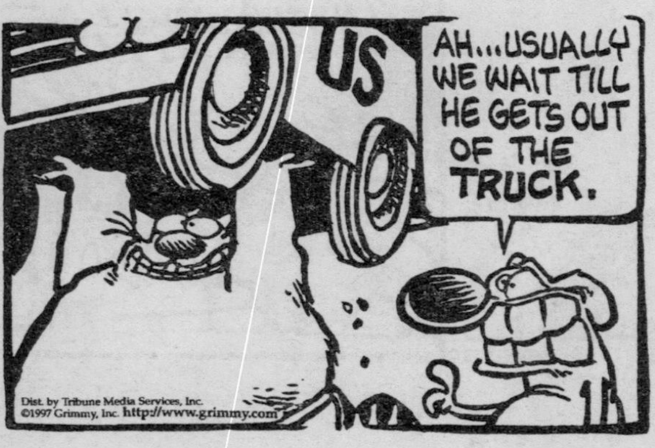
US
AH...USUALLY WE WAIT TILL HE GETS OUT OF THE TRUCK.
Dist. by Tribune Media Services, Inc.
©1997 Grimmy, Inc. http://www.grimmy.com

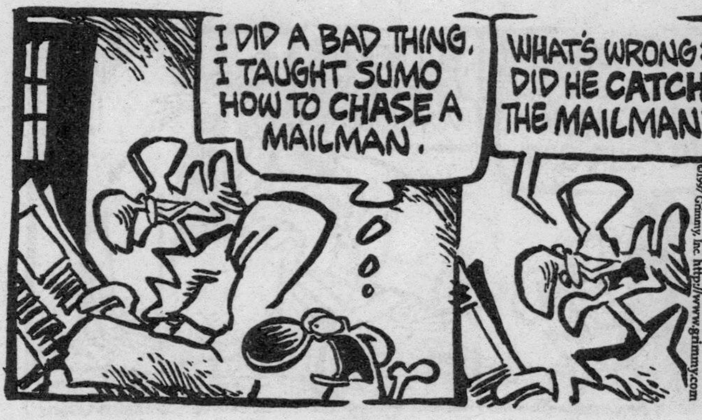
I DID A BAD THING. I TAUGHT SUMO HOW TO CHASE A MAILMAN.
WHAT'S WRONG? DID HE CATCH THE MAILMAN?
Dist. by Tribune Media Services, Inc. ©1997 Grimmy, Inc. http://www.grimmy.com

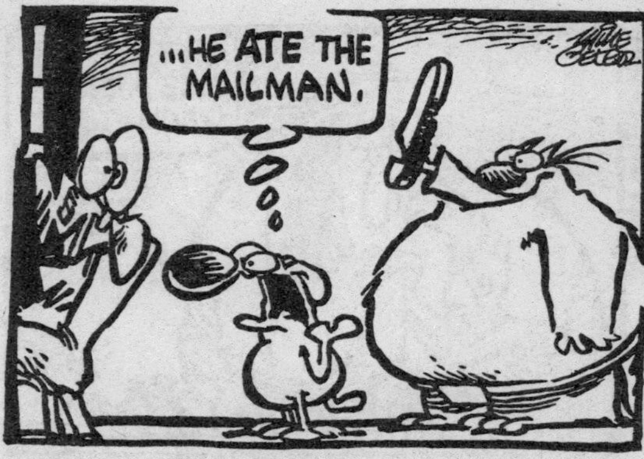
...HE ATE THE MAILMAN.

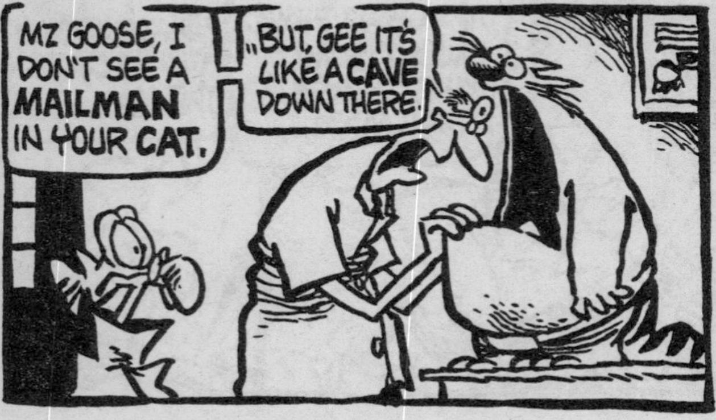
MZ GOOSE, I DON'T SEE A **MAILMAN** IN YOUR **CAT**.
...BUT, GEE IT'S LIKE A **CAVE** DOWN THERE.

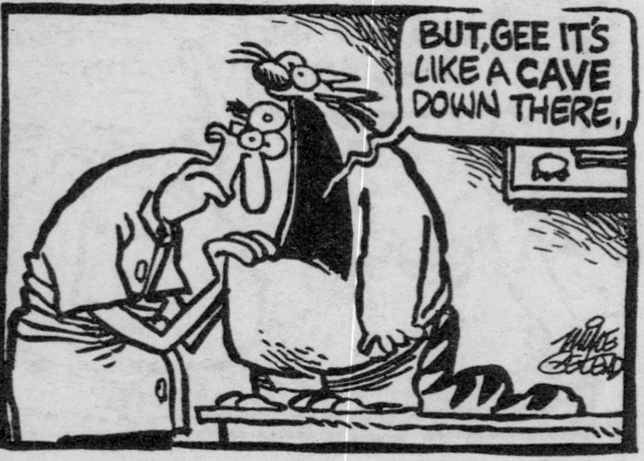
BUT, GEE IT'S LIKE A **CAVE** DOWN THERE,

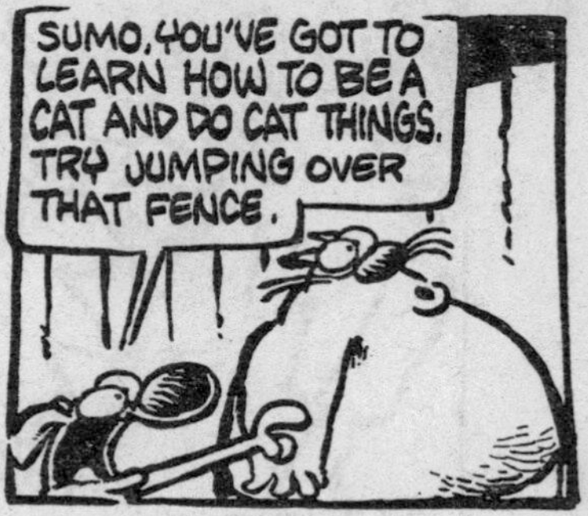
SUMO, YOU'VE GOT TO LEARN HOW TO BE A CAT AND DO CAT THINGS. TRY JUMPING OVER THAT FENCE.

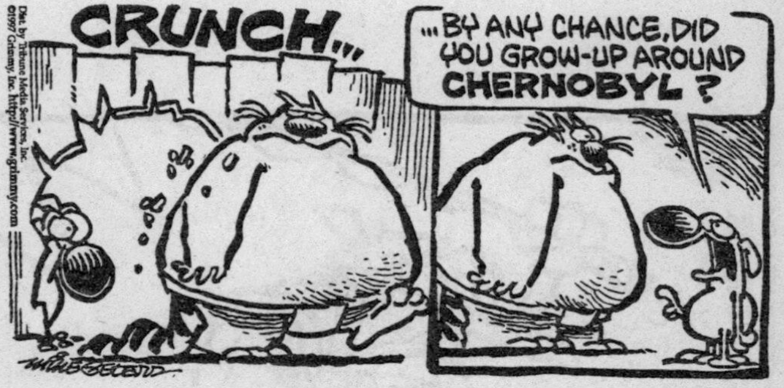
CRUNCH...
...BY ANY CHANCE, DID YOU GROW-UP AROUND CHERNOBYL?
Dist. by Tribune Media Services, Inc.
©1997 Grimmy, Inc. http://www.grimmy.com

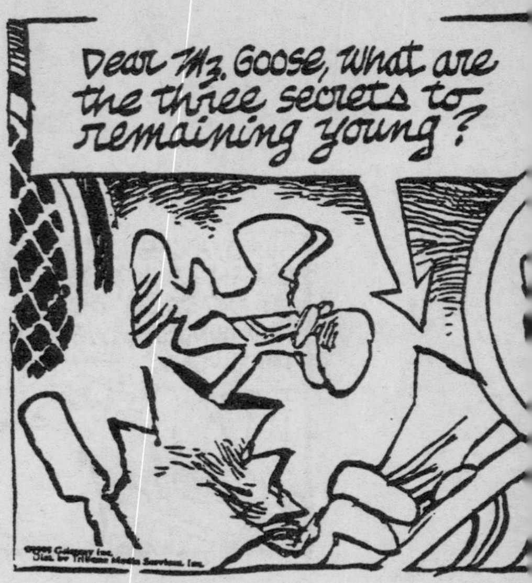
Dear Mz. Goose, What are the three secrets to remaining young?

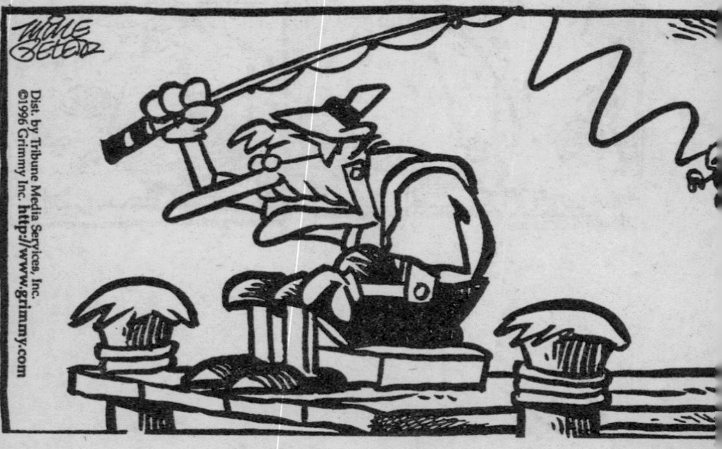
Dist. by Tribune Media Services, Inc.
©1996 Grimmy Inc. http://www.grimmy.com

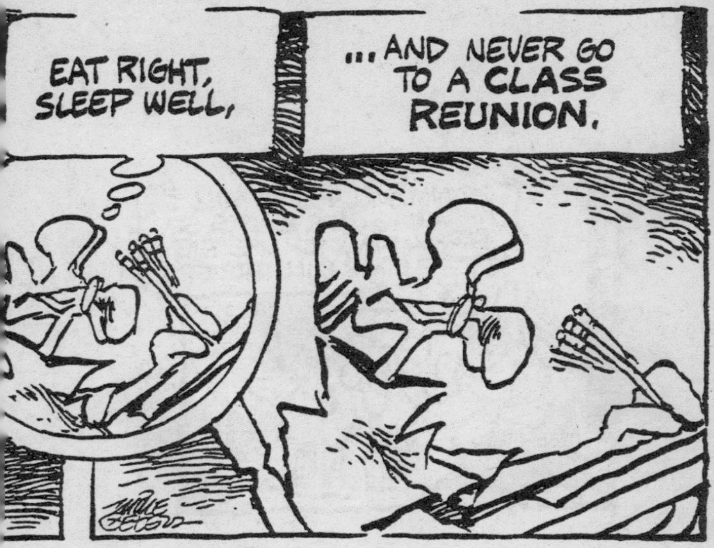
EAT RIGHT, SLEEP WELL,
...AND NEVER GO TO A CLASS REUNION.

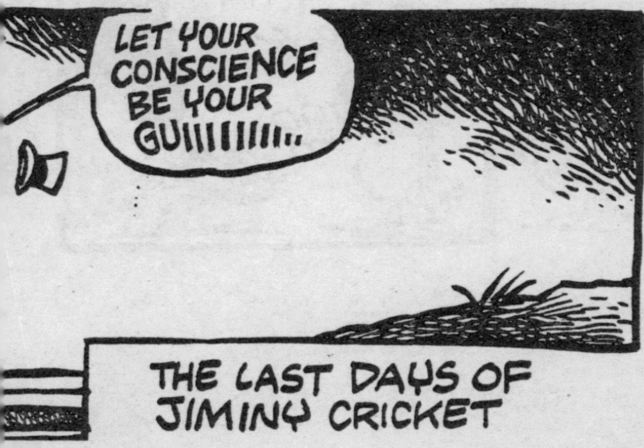
LET YOUR CONSCIENCE BE YOUR GUIIIIIIII..
THE LAST DAYS OF JIMINY CRICKET

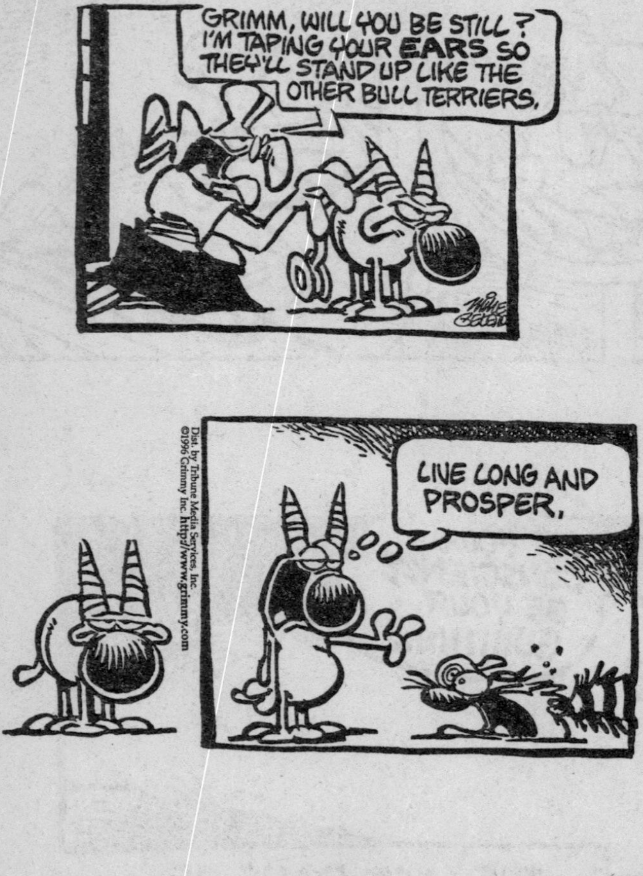
GRIMM, WILL YOU BE STILL? I'M TAPING YOUR EARS SO THEY'LL STAND UP LIKE THE OTHER BULL TERRIERS.
LIVE LONG AND PROSPER.

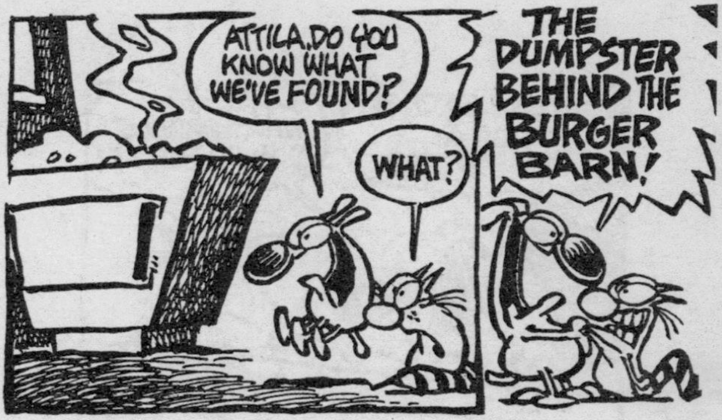
ATTILA, DO YOU KNOW WHAT WE'VE FOUND?
WHAT?
THE DUMPSTER BEHIND THE BURGER BARN!

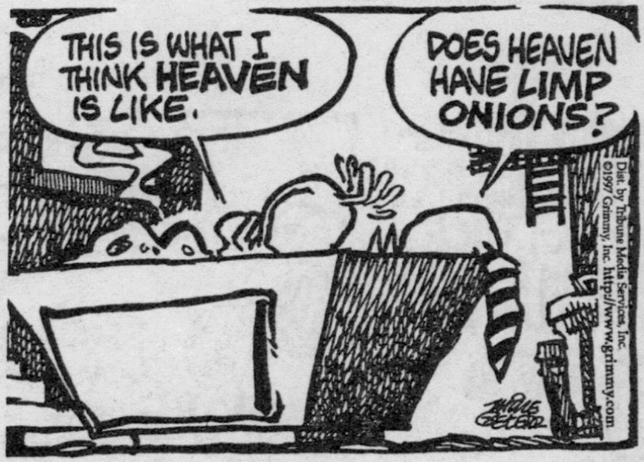
THIS IS WHAT I THINK HEAVEN IS LIKE.
DOES HEAVEN HAVE LIMP ONIONS?
Dist. by Tribune Media Services, Inc.
©1997 Grimmy, Inc. http://www.grimmy.com

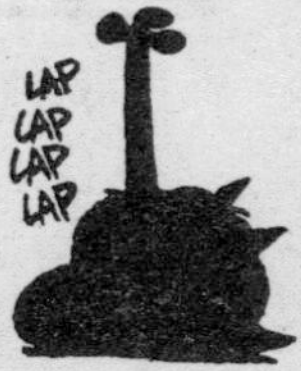
LAP
LAP
LAP
LAP

I LOVE EATING OUT OF A DUMPSTER.
LET'S SEE, WHAT SHOULD I HAVE FIRST?
Dist. by Tribune Media Services, Inc.
©1997 Grimmy, Inc. http://www.grimmy.com

HOW ABOUT TWO ALL-BEEF PATTIES, SPECIAL SAUCE, LETTUCE, ONIONS ON A SESAME SEED BUN?
DO YOU WANT FLIES WITH THAT?

WHAT ARE YOU DOING, GRIMMY?
I'M LOOKING FOR A HAPPY MEAL
I'D SETTLE FOR JUST A MILDLY AMUSING MEAL.
PLOP
Dist. by Tribune Media Services, Inc.
©1997 Grimmy, Inc. http://www.grimmy.com

A DUMPSTER IS A WONDERFUL PLACE TO EAT!
IT'S GOT GREAT FOOD... IT'S INTIMATE... QUIET...
...AND THEY CLEAN HOUSE ONCE A WEEK.
DUMP
Dist. by Tribune Media Services, Inc.
©1997 Grimmy, Inc. http://www.grimmy.com

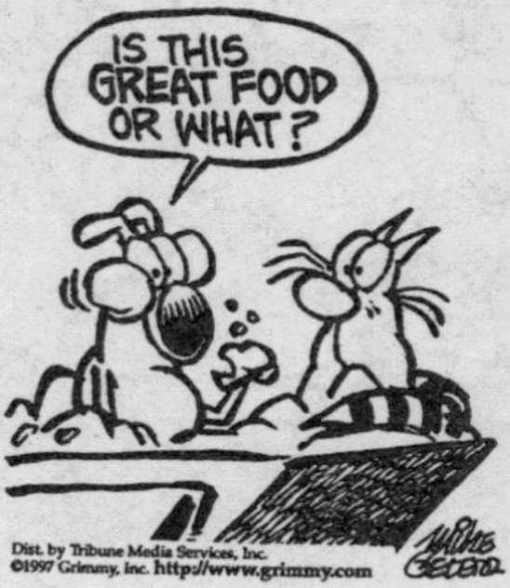
IS THIS GREAT FOOD OR WHAT?
Dist. by Tribune Media Services, Inc.
©1997 Grimmy, Inc. http://www.grimmy.com

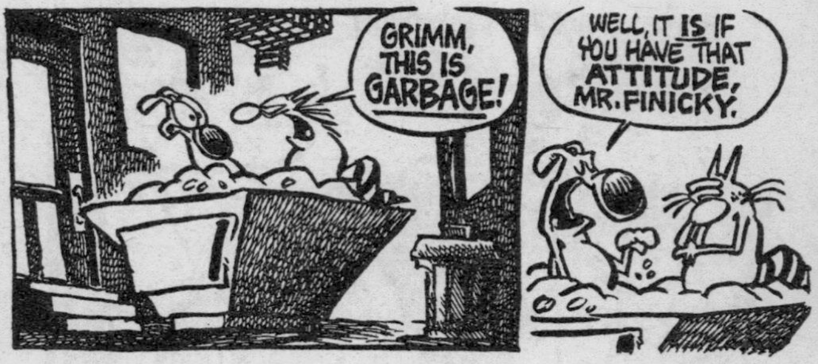
GRIMM, THIS IS GARBAGE!
WELL, IT IS IF YOU HAVE THAT ATTITUDE, MR. FINICKY.

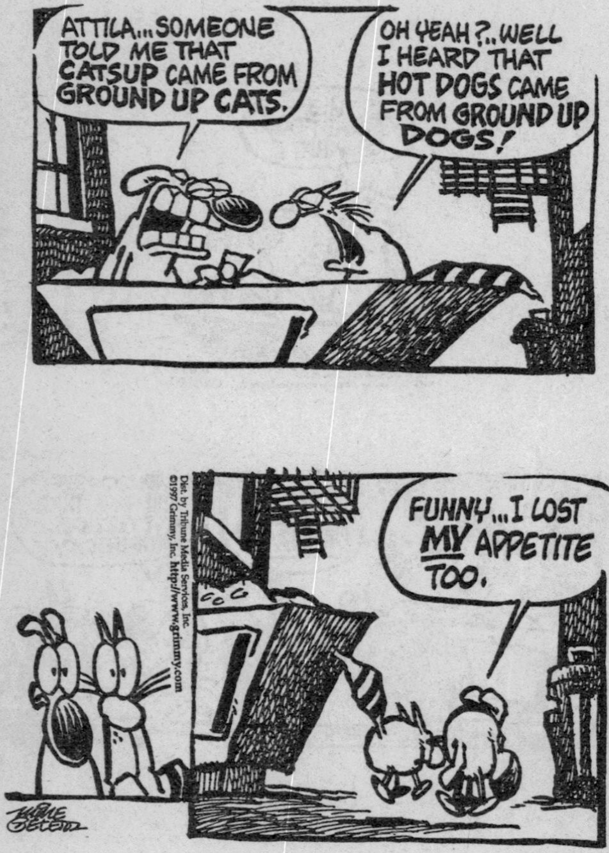
ATTILA...SOMEONE TOLD ME THAT CATSUP CAME FROM GROUND UP CATS.
OH YEAH ?.. WELL I HEARD THAT HOT DOGS CAME FROM GROUND UP DOGS!
FUNNY...I LOST MY APPETITE TOO.
Dist. by Tribune Media Services, Inc.
©1997 Grimmy, Inc. http://www.grimmy.com

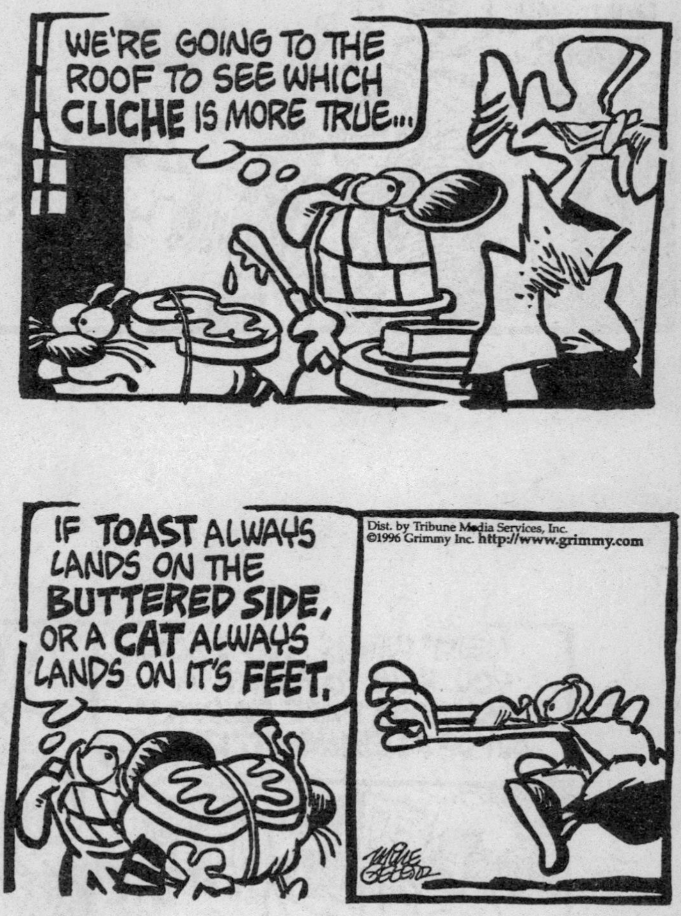
WE'RE GOING TO THE ROOF TO SEE WHICH CLICHE IS MORE TRUE...
IF TOAST ALWAYS LANDS ON THE BUTTERED SIDE, OR A CAT ALWAYS LANDS ON IT'S FEET.
Dist. by Tribune Media Services, Inc.
©1996 Grimmy Inc. http://www.grimmy.com

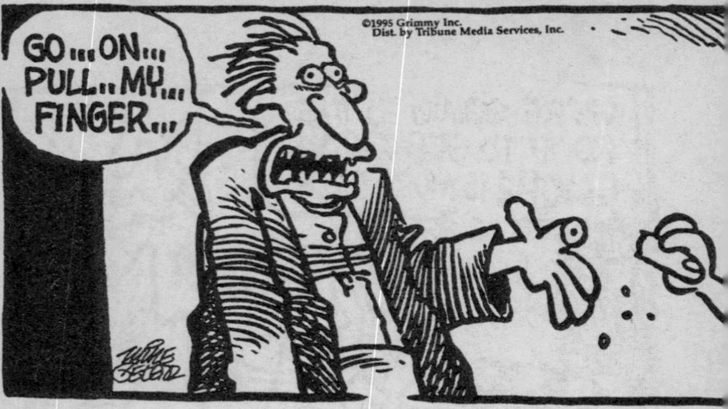
GO... ON... PULL.. MY... FINGER...
©1995 Grimmy Inc.
Dist. by Tribune Media Services, Inc.

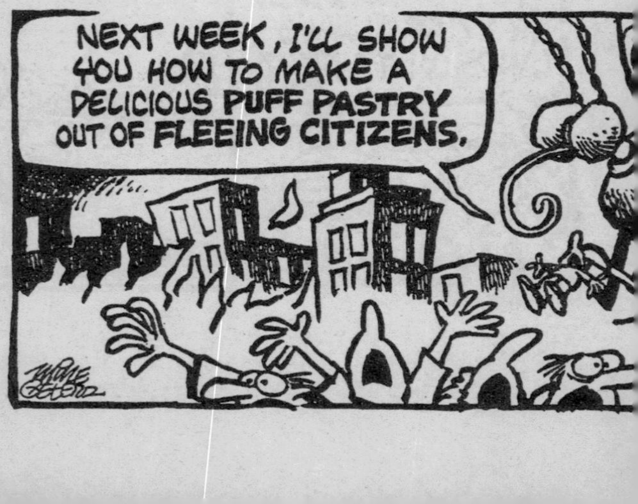
NEXT WEEK, I'LL SHOW YOU HOW TO MAKE A DELICIOUS PUFF PASTRY OUT OF FLEEING CITIZENS.

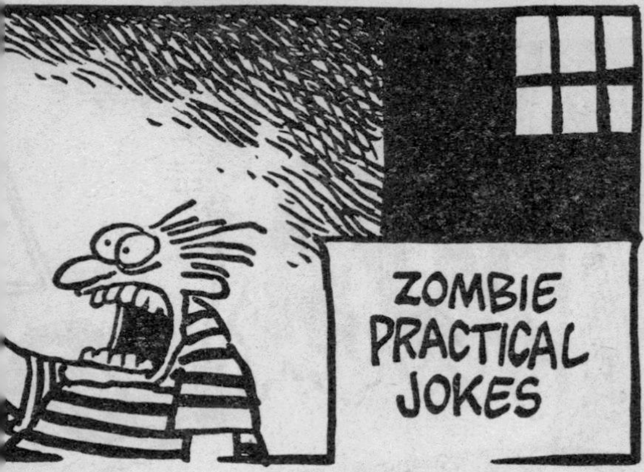
ZOMBIE PRACTICAL JOKES

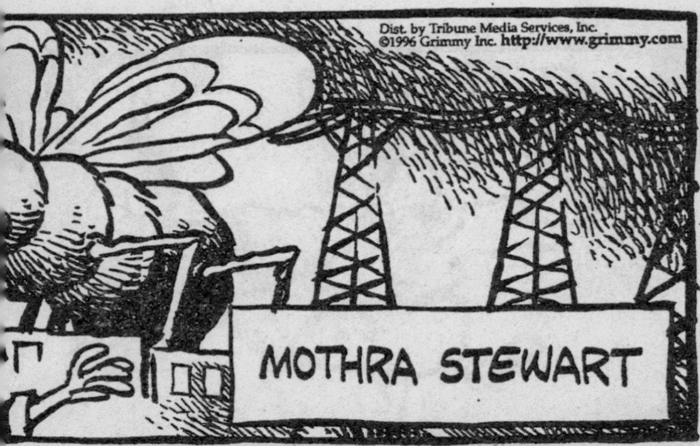
Dist. by Tribune Media Services, Inc.
©1996 Grimmy Inc. http://www.grimmy.com
MOTHRA STEWART

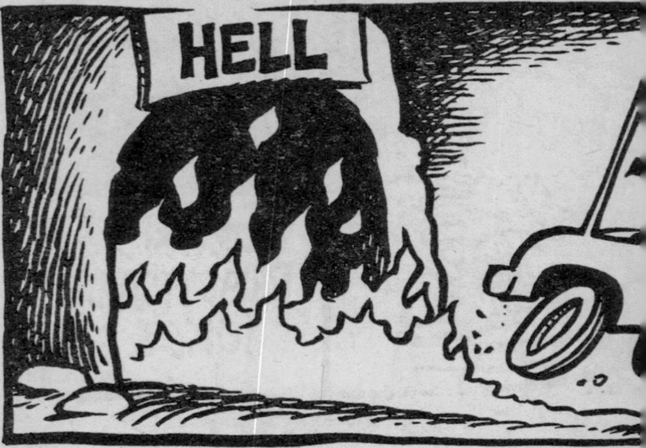
HELL

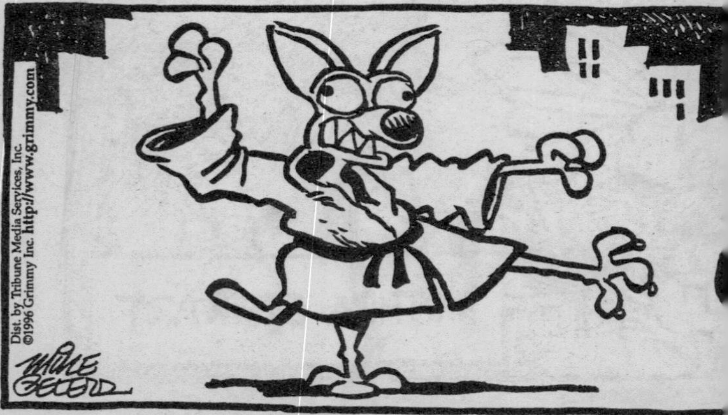
Dist. by Tribune Media Services, Inc.
©1996 Grimmy Inc. http://www.grimmy.com

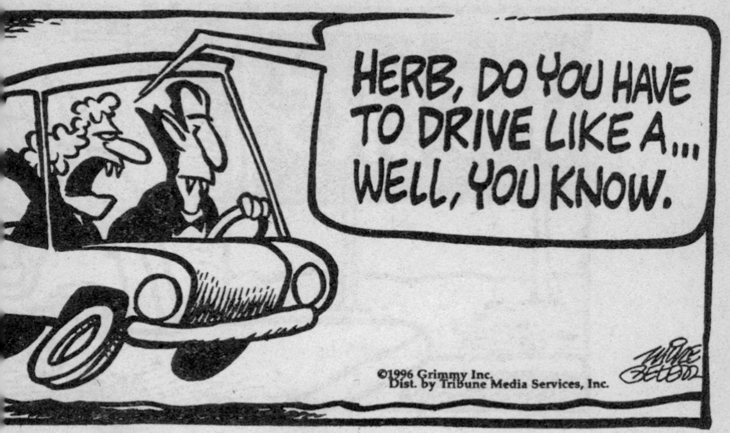
HERB, DO YOU HAVE TO DRIVE LIKE A... WELL, YOU KNOW.
©1996 Grimmy Inc.
Dist. by Tribune Media Services, Inc.

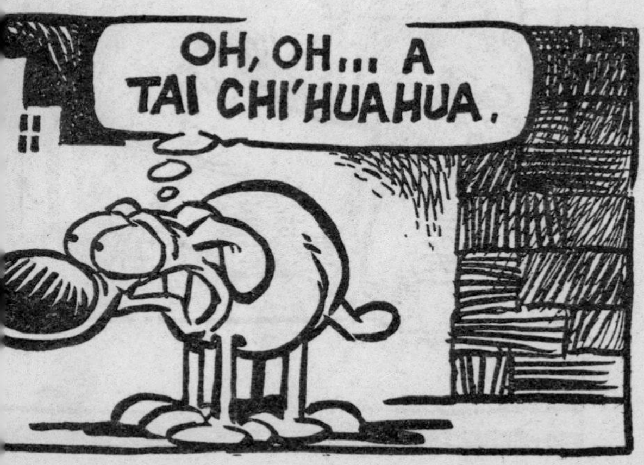
OH, OH... A TAI CHI'HUAHUA.

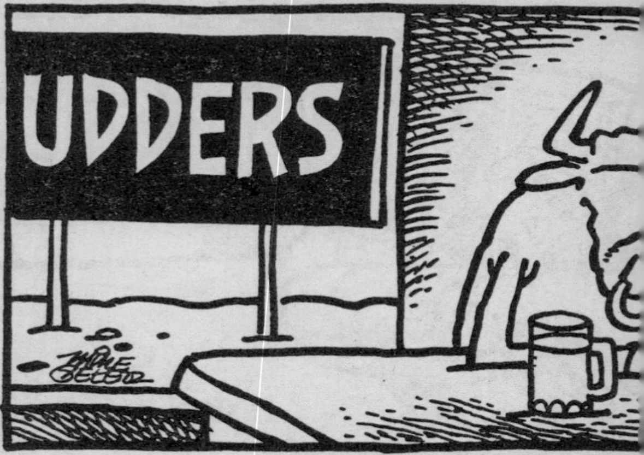
UDDERS

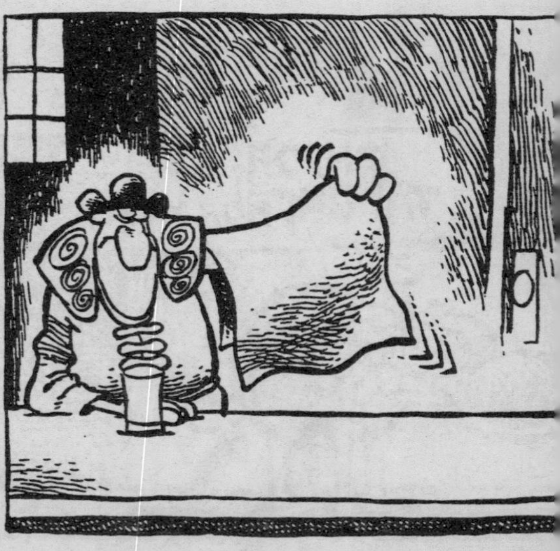

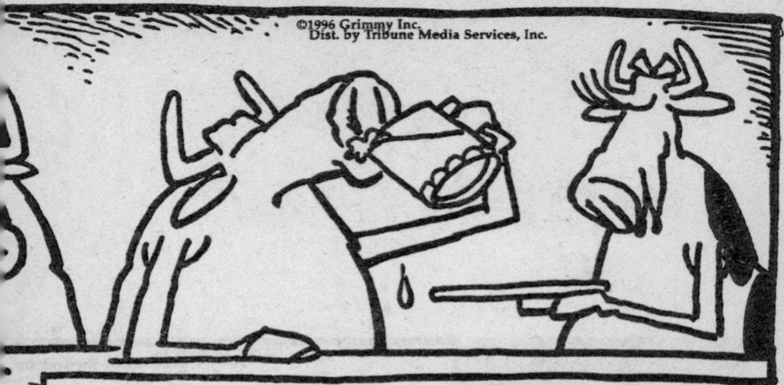
©1996 Grimmy Inc.
Dist. by Tribune Media Services, Inc.

POPULAR BEER JOINT FOR BULLS

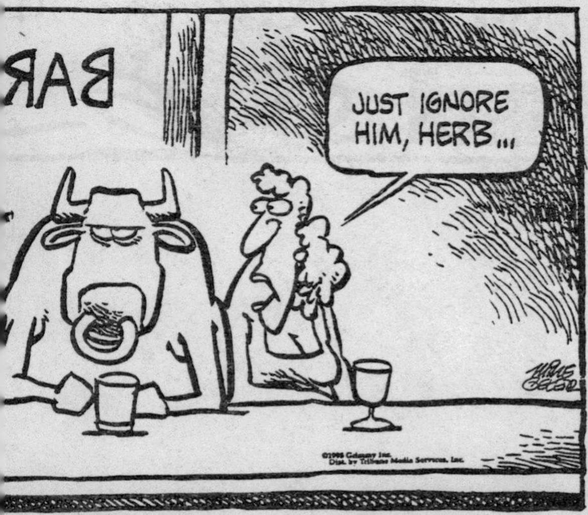
BAR
JUST IGNORE HIM, HERB...

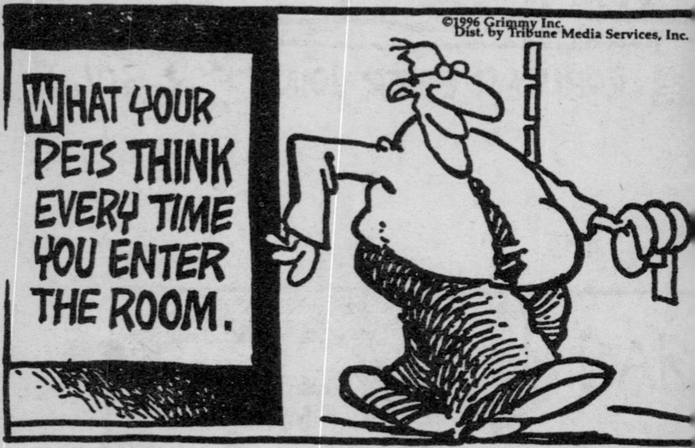
WHAT YOUR PETS THINK EVERY TIME YOU ENTER THE ROOM.
©1996 Grimmy Inc.
Dist. by Tribune Media Services, Inc.

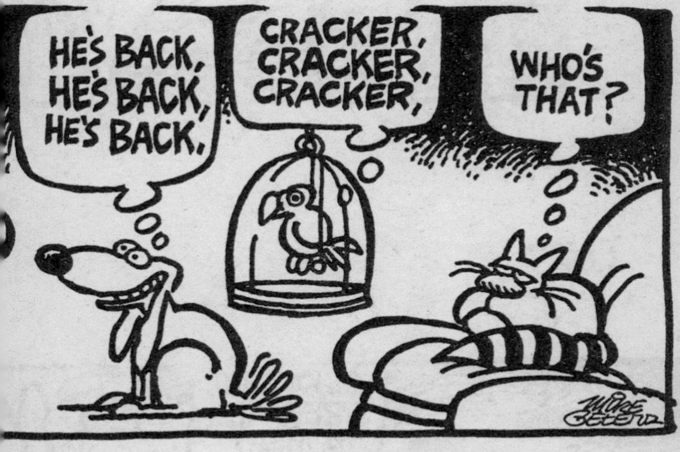
HE'S BACK, HE'S BACK, HE'S BACK,
CRACKER, CRACKER, CRACKER,
WHO'S THAT?

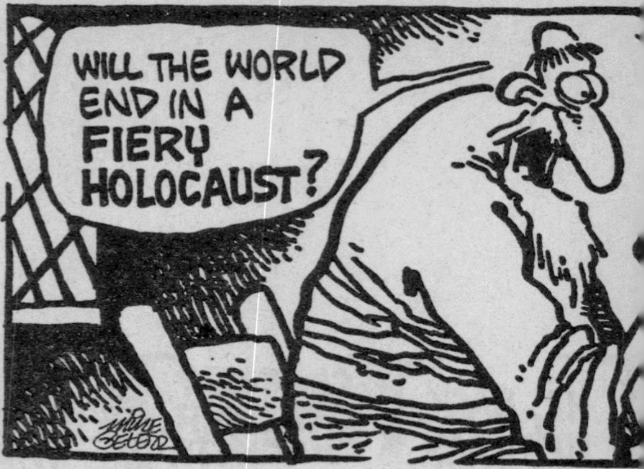
WILL THE WORLD END IN A FIERY HOLOCAUST?

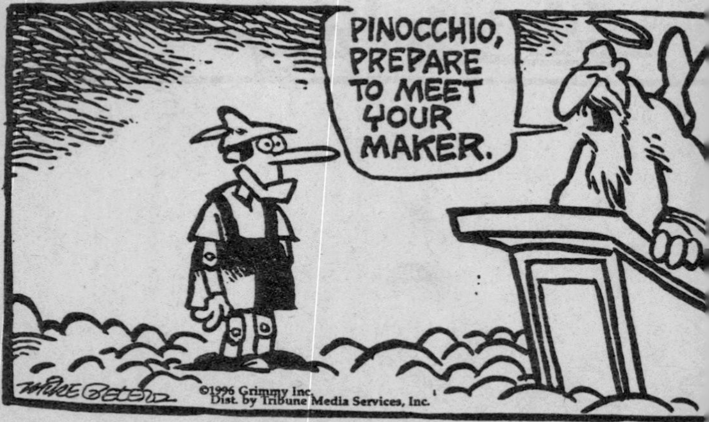
PINOCCHIO, PREPARE TO MEET YOUR MAKER.
©1996 Grimmy Inc.
Dist. by Tribune Media Services, Inc.

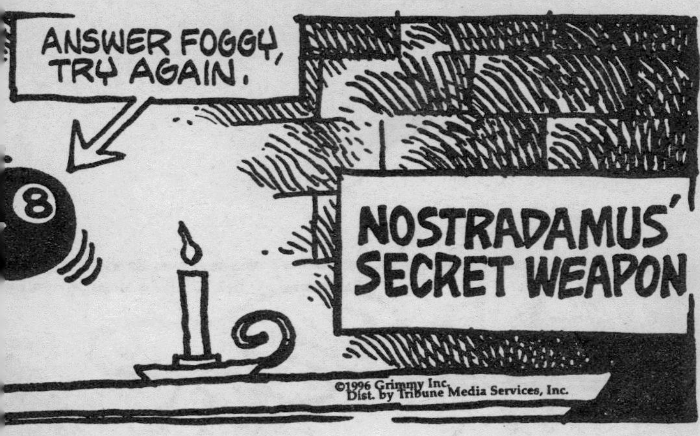
ANSWER FOGGY, TRY AGAIN.
8
NOSTRADAMUS' SECRET WEAPON
©1996 Grimmy Inc.
Dist. by Tribune Media Services, Inc.

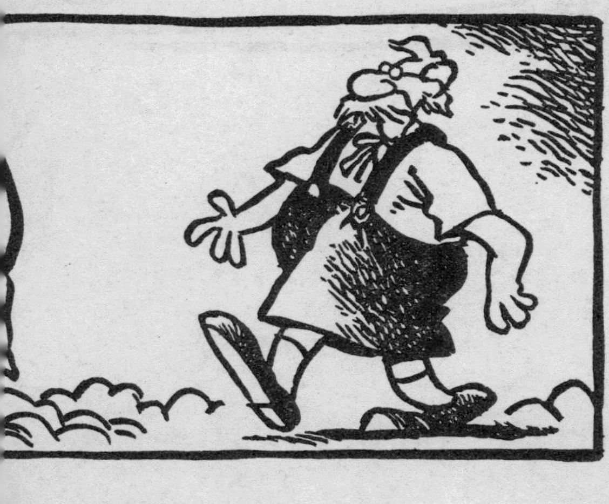

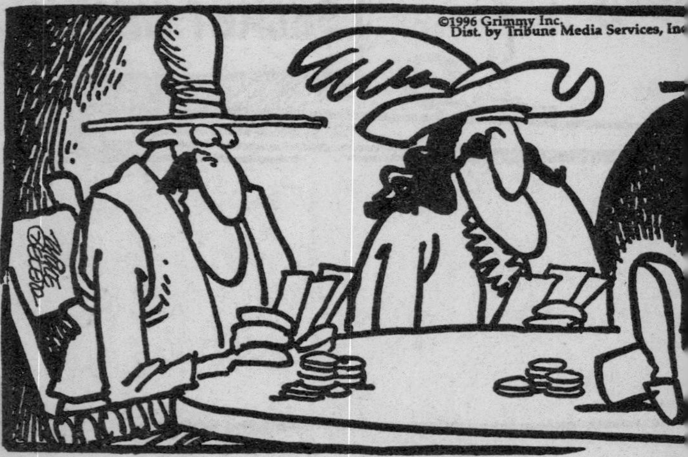
©1996 Grimmy Inc.
Dist. by Tribune Media Services, Inc

THE GAME TOOK AN UGLY TURN WHEN **CAPTAIN HOOK** AND **CAPTAIN AHAB** BET AN **ARM** AND A **LEG.**

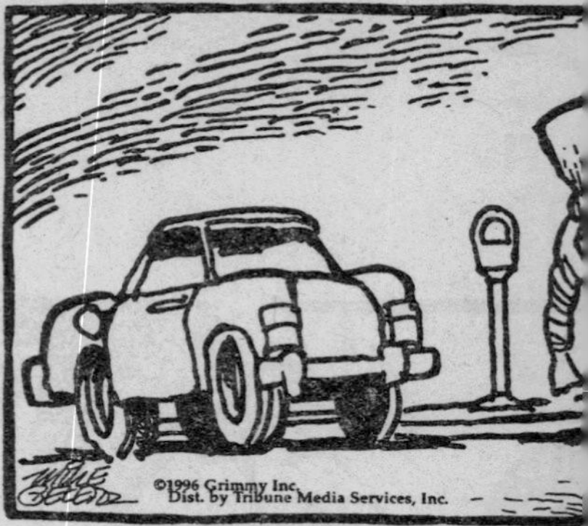
©1996 Grimmy Inc.
Dist. by Tribune Media Services, Inc.

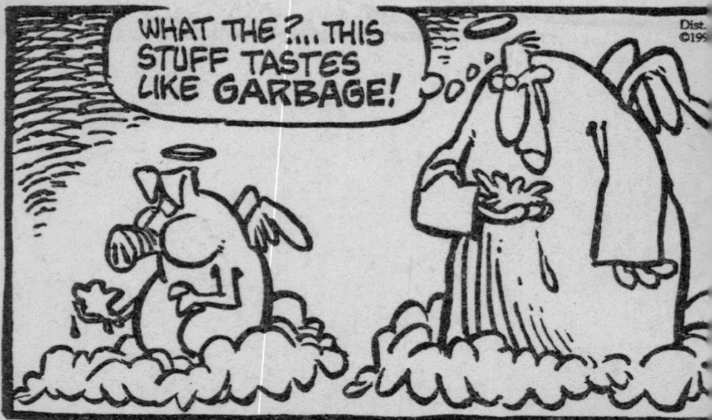
WHAT THE ?... THIS STUFF TASTES LIKE GARBAGE!

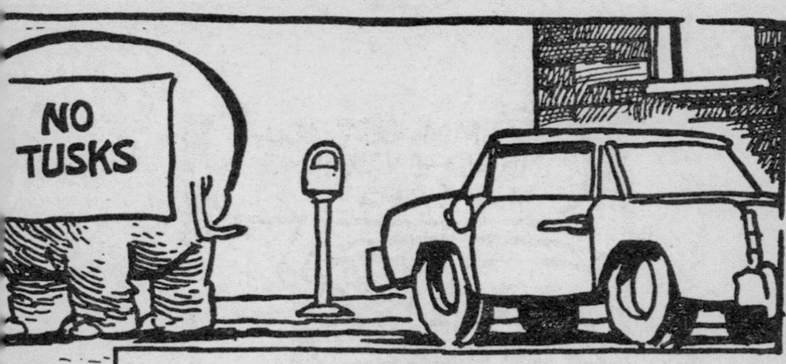
NO
TUSKS

WHEN TARZAN PARKS IN THE CITY

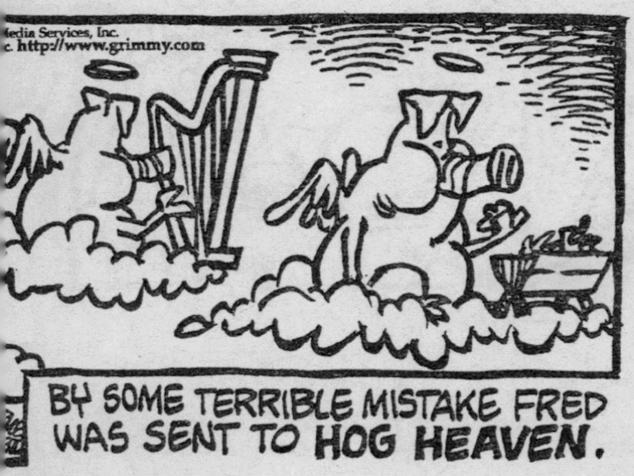
edia Services, Inc.
c. http://www.grimmy.com

BY SOME TERRIBLE MISTAKE FRED
WAS SENT TO **HOG HEAVEN.**

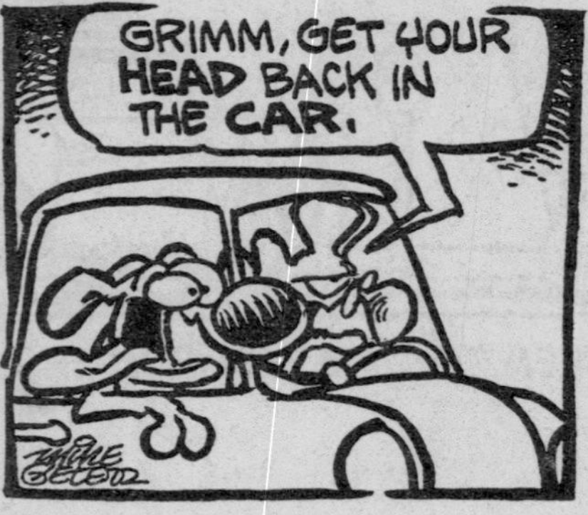
GRIMM, GET YOUR HEAD BACK IN THE CAR.

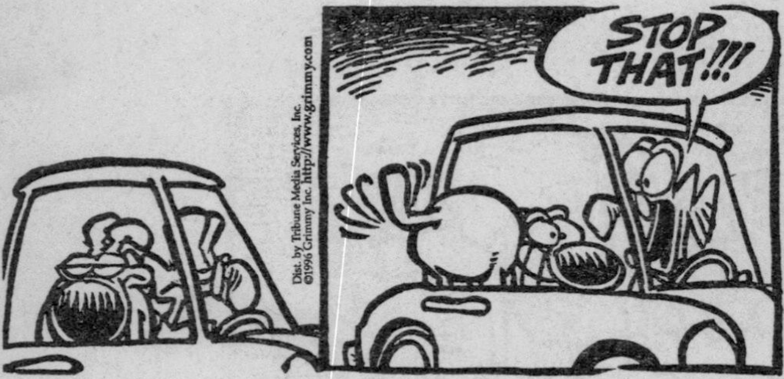
STOP THAT!!!
Dist. by Tribune Media Services, Inc.
©1996 Grimmy Inc. http://www.grimmy.com